ANTICIPATING

Longing for

ANTICIPATING
JESUS' RETURN

DEREK PRINCE

ANTICIPATING JESUS' RETURN
Longing for His Appearing

© 2018 Derek Prince Ministries – International
This edition DPM-UK 2018
All rights reserved.

Published by DPM-UK Kingsfield, PO Box 393, Hitchin, SG5 9EU,
United Kingdom
www.dpmuk.org

ISBN: 978-1-78263-619-9
e-Pub: 978-1-78263-620-5
Kindle: 978-1-78263-621-2
Product Code: B130

Derek Prince Ministries · www.derekprince.com
Set in Arno by Raphael Freeman, Renana Typesetting

Contents

Introduction: Are You Longing?   1

Chapter 1: The Right Perspective   4

Chapter 2: Finishing the Race   9

Chapter 3: Expectancy   17

Chapter 4: The Main Event   25

Chapter 5: Hidden in Christ   33

Chapter 6: Union with Jesus   40

Chapter 7: Union with One Another   49

Chapter 8: Humanity's Only Hope   57

Chapter 9: His Kingdom Come   64

Chapter 10: Redemption of Creation   73

Chapter 11: Nature's Anticipation   86

Chapter 12: How Should We Prepare?   94

Chapter 13: Completing Our Assignment   109

Chapter 14: Continuing Prayer   117

Chapter 15: Hastening His Return   129

Chapter 16: Keeping the Faith   137

Appendix A:
    Comforting the Jewish People   145

Introduction
Are You Longing?

Throughout the many years I have studied the Scriptures, I never cease to be amazed at how practical God is. From even the most spiritual and heavenly themes in the Bible, a practical application always seems to emerge to help us apply biblical principles to our lives here on earth. The subject of this study, *Anticipating Jesus' Return*, is no different. In fact, it is my hope that this theme will do as much for you as it has done for me. In my case, it has changed my entire attitude toward the coming of the Lord.

A Personal Impact
The appearing of Christ and His ultimate return

in glory is one of the greatest events foretold in the Bible. For centuries, it has been the subject of endless scrutiny, debate, and speculation. My purpose in this book, however, is to deal with this topic in a way that is not abstract or theoretical, but extremely practical. It is my intent to show how Christ's return affects us personally – including the way we live in the here and now. It is not simply an event to occur in the unknown future. Rather, the return of Jesus is a vital factor in our lives today.

As I developed the material for this study, the reality of the Lord's return intensified in its importance to me. When the Holy Spirit first impressed this theme upon me, it just lingered for a while in my mind. Over the years, I have seen this "lingering" as an indication that the Lord wanted to show me something deeper on a topic. Gradually, the return of Jesus Christ became the focus of deep meditation and study in the Scriptures, and that process eventually led me to some serious self-examination. Ultimately, I realized that I was being confronted by one of the most important questions I would ever face: *Am I truly longing for the Lord's return?* I will ask you the same question I felt the Lord asking me: *Are you longing for His appearing?*

Right now, you may feel as uncertain about your response to that first question as I felt about mine! However, I believe that as you read this book and contemplate its message, a different answer will begin to take shape in your heart and mind – an answer that will change your outlook on life forever. Shall we get started? There is no time like the present for us to begin *Anticipate Jesus' Return.*

Chapter 1
The Right Perspective

Why should we focus our lives on the appearing or return of the Lord Jesus Christ? We see one reason in the example of the early Church.

From my study of the Bible, I have come to believe that the attitude of the early Church toward the anticipated appearing of the Lord was one of the major forces motivating them toward the rapid spread of the gospel. In contrast, I have come to see that the modern Church's lack of the same attitude is one of the reasons it is so tepid and unsuccessful in its mission in the world today.

Bearing that contrast in mind, let's examine this important subject. I want to emphasize what I said earlier – that our approach to the topic will not be abstract or theoretical but extremely practical. We will see how it affects us personally, right down to influencing the very way we live. I offer this book in the hope that this theme will do as much for you as it has done for me. Let's begin by asking the key question one more time: *Are you longing for His appearing?*

Paul's Example

The Apostle Paul provides a pointed example for us. When Paul was facing the end of his life, he wrote one of the most touching passages in all of Scripture, found in Second Timothy 4:6–8. At the time, Paul was a prisoner in Rome, facing trial and ultimate execution at the hands of the emperor Nero. It is important for us to realize that Nero was perhaps the most wicked ruler in all of human history – a totally ungodly, unrighteous man. This information enables us to better understand the significance of Paul's words in the light of that wicked situation.

For I am already being poured out as a drink offering, and the time of my departure is at hand. I have fought the good fight, I have finished the race, I have kept the faith. Finally, there is laid up for me the crown of righteousness, which the Lord, the righteous Judge, will give to me on that Day, and not to me only but also to all who have loved His appearing.

A Time of Release

What Paul says in this remarkable passage relates directly to many aspects of our study of the theme, *Anticipating Jesus' Return.* As he waits in prison, contemplating his execution, Paul is both looking back over his life and forward to eternity. In essence, he is saying "farewell" to Timothy and to us, with some of the most important words he has ever written. Bearing that in mind, we need to examine this passage more closely, beginning with the first verse. Here, Paul is sharing with us his thoughts in the present moment:

For I am already being poured out as a drink offering, and the time for my departure is at hand (2 Timothy 4:6).

As I studied the Greek text for this verse, it struck me that a better translation for the word *departure* would be *release*. The word *departure* does not carry the sense of what kind of departure Paul was anticipating. It might be a good departure, or it might be a bad departure. But the word *release* suggests that Paul was yearning for his release from his body – the body in which he had served the Lord so faithfully for so many years.

A Life Poured Out

I love Paul's plaintive words, *"For I am already being poured out as a drink offering."* A drink offering was one of the sacrificial offerings of the Levitical priesthood, mainly described in the book of Leviticus. As a devout Jew, Paul was very aware that there were primary offerings of slain animals and birds, and there were other offerings such as grain or baked flour. What Paul also knew was that with nearly all offerings, God ordained that there should also be a drink offering – a certain portion of wine poured out together with the particular offering or sacrifice.

When Paul was thinking and speaking of

himself and his life, his mind was on this drink offering. He was envisioning his own life blood being poured out in martyrdom. Such a "drink offering" would seal the offering that he had already been bringing to God – the offering of the fruits of his ministry.

I want to suggest that there really are very few offerings that have significance or that are acceptable to God unless they are accompanied by the drink offering of a life poured out. If you analyze the ministries that have really changed the world and deeply affected the lives of people, you find a consistent factor – with every one of those ministries, somebody had to pour out his or her life. They were not necessarily martyrs, but in the selfless giving of themselves their lives were like a drink offering, "poured out." In the same way, our service to the Lord – no matter how noble – needs to be offered up as a drink offering – a life poured out.

Chapter 2
Finishing the Race

In our study of Paul's profound words in 2 Timothy, we shift from his focus on the present to his recollection and evaluation of the past. We see this in verse 7, where Paul pens what I believe are some of the most triumphant words ever written by a human being.

Bear in mind the reality of his situation. He was getting on in years. He was somewhat infirmed. He was facing winter conditions and he was evidently cold in the damp prison. He did not have sufficient clothing. (We know this because he sent an urgent message to Timothy to bring a cloak with him when he came.) In addition, Paul was completely alone. Most of his close associates had forsaken him.

By the world's standards, Paul's life was ending in complete failure. However, he knew the world's standard of success was not the ultimate standard. That is why, as Paul faces the end of life, there is not a single hint of defeat or regret anywhere in this epistle. Instead, he declares these words of triumph:

> *I have fought the good fight, I have finished the race, I have kept the faith* (2 Timothy 4:7).

For 2,000 years, these words have given believers strength, courage, and determination to endure until the end. Each statement is in the perfect tense in Greek. *It is done. It is complete.* I would like to suggest to you that if you want to finish your race and if you want to keep the faith, you are going to have to fight the fight! Conflict is a major aspect of the Christian life. I have said many times that I think you can get to heaven without theology. I am not sure you will get there without courage. Coming to the end of life in victory is more a test of your character than of your intellect.

The Crown of Righteousness

Having spoken of the present and reflected on the past, Paul then turns his attention toward the future – toward eternity. Paul begins verse 8 of 2 Timothy with these words:

Finally, there is laid up for me the crown of righteousness.

The word *crown* used here is not referring to a royal diadem worn by kings. In the New Testament there are two words translated as "crown." One is the Greek word for *diadem,* which is a jeweled crown worn as a royal mark of kingship. Revelation tells us that when Jesus appears, on His head are many crowns, or diadems, because He is the King of all kings. He alone has the right to wear every crown.

The word Paul uses in verse 8, however, is for the other kind of crown, which is a reference to the Olympic games of those days. This kind of crown was a laurel wreath – just a simple sprig of laurel, which was placed upon the brow of the one who had won a contest, very similar in nature to the gold medals of our Olympics today.

So, in a way, if you wanted to modernize Paul's statement, he was saying, "From now on I'm expecting my gold medal, because I have won my contest!"

After this initial thought, Paul continues in verse 8, introducing a very important perspective for us.

> *Finally, there is laid up for me a crown of righteousness, which the Lord, the righteous Judge, will give to me on that Day.*

Notice Paul's emphasis that the Lord is "the righteous Judge." Why did Paul call attention to this fact? Because he was appearing before Nero, a very unrighteous judge who gave him a very unjust and brutal sentence. But Paul was looking forward to another judgement, where he would receive a crown of righteousness. In effect, Paul was saying, "Nero doesn't have the last word. There's one more judgment to come that will be totally righteous and just. It will be before the Lord, the righteous Judge." Paul knew what the Lord would give him on that day. A crown of righteousness. But there is more to be said on that.

Loving His Appearing

In the context of a life poured out in the present, a completion of purpose in the past, and the anticipated reward in his future, Paul comes to the phrase which so deeply gripped me over the years. It is the concept that is the theme of this book, *Anticipating Jesus' Return*. We will look at the entire passage again, and then turn our focus to the section I have highlighted.

> *For I am already being poured out as a drink offering, and the time of my departure is at hand. I have fought the good fight, I have finished the race, I have kept the faith. Finally, there is laid up for me the crown of righteousness, which the Lord, the righteous Judge, will give to me on that Day,* **and not to me only but also to all who have loved His appearing** (2 Timothy 4:6–8).

As you can see, the New King James Version of this verse reads, "to all who have loved His appearing." This is an accurate translation, but the New International Version reads Longing for His Appearing, which I think conveys a little more intensity in its meaning.

A Special Group

The word used for *love* in the New King James Version is *agapao*, which is the strong word for intense love. Paul writes it in the perfect tense, which describes a settled, committed attitude. Maybe the best way to express this is to say, "You are in love with this thought." Paul is writing about those who are "in love with" the appearing of the Lord in His glory.

As I studied this very significant aspect of this verse, I saw that within the Body of Christ, God recognizes a special group of believers. What sets this group apart? They are marked out by the fact that they are truly in love with the appearing of Jesus. For those special believers, God has a special honor – the crown of righteousness. Evidently, this crown is not going to be given to all believers. Rather, it is going to be given only to those believers who, in this life, have passionately loved – or longed for – the return of the Lord Jesus. I am very careful about singling out special groups of believers within the Church. (Sometimes special groups can become special problems!) But here we have a special group which is authenticated by the word of God. It is as if God looks all through the body of Christ and says, *"There* is a sister who is longing for my appearing. *There* is a brother who is longing for my appearing." Then He says to the angels (or whoever is responsible for this part of the administration of heaven), "Be sure to prepare for them a crown of righteousness."

Do We Qualify?

As I meditated on these truths I was studying, I had to examine my own life. I had to ask myself: *Do I qualify? Do I have the mark of one who has loved His appearing?* Then I thought about the many Christians I had met throughout the years of my ministry, and I said to myself: *How many of them qualify?*

I came to this conclusion: I don't know many who have that distinguishing mark – who seem to be in love with the appearing of the Lord.

What about you? How would you answer for yourself? *Do you qualify for that special honor?*

In this study, it is my hope that as we examine this issue together in the helpful light of Scripture, the Holy Spirit will help us. He will enable us to address and to answer this most important question: *Are we longing for His appearing?*

Chapter 3
Expectancy

Throughout the New Testament, there is an unmistakable, vibrant anticipation for Christ's appearing. Yet somehow, most Christians today don't have that same sense of expectation. Why aren't we motivated to think about the Lord's return? Why isn't it as important to us as it was to the early Church?

In this chapter, we will begin to explore solutions to this dilemma by turning to the Scriptures, beginning with Titus 2:11–13:

> *For the grace of God that brings salvation has appeared to all men, teaching us that, denying ungodliness and worldly lusts, we should live*

soberly, righteously, and godly in the present age, looking for the blessed hope and glorious appearing of our great God and Savior Jesus Christ.

Grace, Paul writes, is "teaching us." (Did you know that grace teaches us?) Many people believe grace is just something you receive, and that is all there is to it! Most would agree that grace is free. You receive it freely, and you cannot earn it. However, there is more to it than that. Once you have received grace, it imposes obligations on you.

You may find yourself reacting: "Obligations? But you just said grace is free!"

Yes, grace is free – but it is not cheap. There is a great difference between being free and being cheap. Paul said that God's grace has appeared, teaching us that *"denying ungodliness and worldly lusts, we should live soberly, righteously, and godly, in the present age."* Without a doubt, those are not "cheap" requirements.

Distinctly Different

Grace teaches us how we should live. Clearly, we should not be living like the people of this world. We should live in a way that is totally different. However, I am not sure that most of God's people in much of the Western world are living distinctly different lives from those around them. Could part of the problem be that we are not as expectant as we should be for the Lord's return?

Someone once handed me a national survey by a secular marketing firm. The survey was not in any way spiritually motivated, but its object was to determine how to sell products to "born-again" Christians.

The accepted estimate was that there were 50 million born-again Christians in the United States. At the time, that was about one-fifth of the population. Such a sizable group would represent a major consumer-market – certainly worthy of study. These secular business professionals wanted to know what to say or do to sell consumer goods to born-again Christians. I could see immediately that it was a very penetrating survey, accurately defining "born-again" Christians.

Actually, the final results were rather disturbing. Here was the conclusion of these marketers:

there was no difference between the born-again Christians and other consumers who made no claim to be born again. Both groups seemed to be motivated in the same way, responding to the same enticements and impulses, because their standards were basically the same.

That is not grace. Grace makes people different.

The Ultimate Motivation

What is the real motivation for a Christian to live a distinctly different life from the world? I believe Paul answers that question in verse 13 of Titus 2:

> *Looking for the blessed hope, and glorious appearing of our great God and Savior Jesus Christ.*

What Paul outlines in the above phrase is the ultimate motivation for the way we live. It is an active anticipation of the coming of the Lord. If we analyze the New Testament, we discover that nearly every appeal to holy living is related to the eager expectation of the Lord's return. I would suggest that where the Church is not living in that expectation, its standards of holiness will always be below those of the New Testament. Somehow, we have lost that motivation.

In the passage above, Paul refers to Jesus' return as "the blessed hope." Perhaps as you are reading this you may be feeling rather hopeless. That feeling of hopelessness may be the result of only looking at your life as it is at this time. Right now, you may be suffering economic, physical, or relational problems. Consequently, as you look out across the horizon of your life, you do not see much cause for hope.

Our "Uplook"

Another part of that same hopelessness may be that you are looking in the wrong direction. Our outlook may be dark – but our "uplook" is always bright. No Christian should have to live in hopelessness. Only the unconverted should be hopeless. If we are looking in the wrong direction, focused totally on living like the world – like the born-again Christians in the survey – we will labor under the problems of the world. In that respect, hopelessness is one of the main problems of our generation today. But for us, that problem can be remedied by our "uplook" – focusing instead upon "the blessed hope."

Please notice in this passage that Paul calls Jesus *"our great God and Savior."* This distinction is very important. Why? Because Jesus is God. If you are not willing to call Him God, I question whether you can call Him Savior – because ultimately, only God can save us. Isaiah 12:2 says, *"Behold, God is my salvation."* Whatever your present circumstances, please realize that nothing and no one except God can save you. The Church cannot save you; the law cannot save you; morality cannot save you. It takes God in the person of Jesus to save you.

Two Unbreakable Appointments

Another Scripture which echoes our theme of looking to the return of Jesus Christ is Hebrews 9:27–29:

> *And as it is appointed for men to die once, but after this the judgment, so Christ was offered once to bear the sins of many. To those who eagerly wait for Him He will appear a second time, apart from sin, for salvation.*

I want to point out two significant truths in this passage. First, every person has two appointments they must keep. You may break every appointment you make on earth, but there are two you are going to keep. Number one is dying. Number two is appearing before the judgment seat of God.

You and I are going to face an eternal judgment. But if we have received Christ as our Savior who forgives our sins, and we have served Him faithfully, it is a judgment we do not need to fear! You and I can actually look forward to it, because we will receive our reward – not condemnation. Therefore, in view of this reality, you and I must live in the light of those two appointments – dying and appearing before the judgment seat.

My second point in regard to this passage in Hebrews takes the form of a question: When Jesus comes back, to whom will He appear? To those who eagerly wait for Him. You and I must ask ourselves if we are in the category of those who are waiting *eagerly*. The New Testament record is very clear: the eager anticipation of the Lord's return is *a foundational motivation for godly living.* If this is so, we would do well to also consider the following question: *What is it about the Lord's appearing that should cause us to be "in love" with it?*

In my study of the New Testament on this subject, I have found four main reasons to be very excited about the return of the Lord Jesus! In the next chapter, we will discuss the first reason, which may come as a surprise to you. However, I intend to provide a solid, scriptural basis for this surprising first reason.

Chapter 4
The Main Event

Our lives are often filled with many important, wonderful events – falling in love, getting married, having your first child, or getting your first job, to name a few. But for Christians, there is an event which is going to happen to you and me which stands far above these milestones in life. In fact, it is the first reason we should be longing for His appearing.

What is that event? Our resurrection. That answer may surprise you. Why? Because as I have already pointed out, most believers today aren't interested in the resurrection, much less living in anticipation of it. In this chapter I want to help you understand why the resurrection will be one of the most – if not *the* most – momentous occasions in our lives. It is clearly the first reason we should be *Anticipating Jesus' Return*.

Understanding the Resurrection

The resurrection is the consummation of our personal salvation. The word *consummate* means to *bring to completion*. Jesus' work on the cross was not complete until He was resurrected. In the same way, our salvation is not complete, or consummated, until we, too, have received our resurrection body. The consummation of our salvation will be the transformation of our physical body, which will be like Jesus' body after His resurrection. All of this will come about at the moment of Christ's appearing in glory.

I have always been very impressed by Paul's singular motivation for living, stated it in the third chapter of Philippians. I believe if you can read this passage with an open mind, it will give you a new perspective regarding your salvation.

You see, many Christians today tend to think the end of our salvation is dying and going to heaven. This is merely one stage, and it is very important. But it is not the end. There is something even more important beyond going to heaven. Paul writes about this in Philippians 3:8–11:

> *Yet indeed I also count all things loss for the excellence of the knowledge of Christ Jesus my Lord, for whom I have suffered the loss of all things, and count them as rubbish, that I may gain Christ and be found in Him, not having my own righteousness, which is from the law, but that which is through faith in Christ, the righteousness which is from God by faith; that I may know Him and the power of His resurrection, and the fellowship of His sufferings, being conformed to His death, if, by any means, I may attain to the resurrection from the dead.*

What was Paul's aim? Toward what end was all his motivation directed? Knowing Christ, sharing His suffering, and sharing His glory, certainly. But the culmination is in these words, *"If, by any means, I may attain to the resurrection from the dead."*

No Matter What the Cost

The phrase "by any means" could alternatively be translated "somehow." Paul is saying, "If *somehow* I may make it through to the resurrection." That statement indicates to me that Paul gives tremendous priority to attaining to his resurrection. No matter what it would cost him, no matter the obstacles, that was his aim – to make it through to the resurrection of the dead.

Paul uses an unusual word here for "resurrection" which means the "*out* resurrection." In other words, he is not referring to the general resurrection of all the dead (saved and unsaved) but to the resurrection which Revelation calls "the first resurrection." Concerning this matter, Scripture says: *"Blessed and holy is he who has a part in the first resurrection"* (Revelation 20:6).

Then Paul goes on to make it very clear that he has not yet attained to this resurrection at the time of his writing.

> *Not that I have already attained, or am already perfected: but I press on, that I may lay hold of that for which Christ Jesus has also laid hold of me* (Philippians 3:12).

It is very apparent that Paul had a purpose and goal in his life. Nothing distresses me more than to meet Christians who are aimless – just drifting, carried to and fro by the currents of life. In contrast to that type of person, Paul had a definite, positive, specific aim. Furthermore, he united his purpose with the Lord's purpose for him.

The apostle John wrote: *"But he who does the will of God abides forever"* (1 John 2:17). What happens when you make God's will your will? You become unsinkable, unshakable, and undefeatable!

The Coming Transformation

Toward the end of Philippians 3, Paul explains what he means by all this – and why he believes all of it to be so important.

> *For our citizenship is in heaven, from which we also eagerly wait for the Savior, the Lord Jesus Christ, who will transform our lowly body that it may be conformed to His glorious body, according to the working by which He is able even to subdue all things to Himself* (Philippians 3:20–21).

It is important for us to realize that we are residents on earth, but our citizenship is in heaven. Please notice again that Paul says, like the writer of Hebrews, "we eagerly wait." Eagerly awaiting the Lord's return is an attitude that is continually emphasized in various parts of the New Testament.

From the passage above, we see that the transformation of our "lowly body" is both the culmination of Philippians 3 and the fulfillment of Paul's purpose. Paul is saying that now, at the present time, we have a "lowly" body – literally, a body of "humiliation." The key word that describes this body is the word *corruption* or *corruptible* (1 Corinthians 15:42, 50–54). However, the transformation Paul is looking toward in this verse is the change of our lowly body to a body of glory – like the glorious body of the resurrected Lord Jesus.

Our Lowly Bodies

It doesn't matter whether you and I are healthy, wealthy, and strong. Regardless of our condition, as a result of man's fall you and I are living in a body of humiliation. The humiliation of that body is manifested for us in many ways.

You and I may be able to afford eating in the finest restaurants, enjoying the choicest steaks. But we all know what will happen at some point. Each of us will have to go to the bathroom. That in itself is a continual reminder of our humiliation.

A woman may put on the sweetest perfume and make herself look absolutely delightful. But if she has to run around getting hot and flustered, she will start to perspire. For both men and women, that perspiration is just a little token of our humiliation.

It is also a fact that the older we become, the more our bodies humble us. Why? Our bodies are lowly because we rebelled against our Creator – and our earthly body is a continual reminder of that fact. It is in this humbled body that we must live until we die or Jesus returns.

Paul tells us, however, that this is not to be our permanent condition. According to the Word, we are going to get a new body – one which will be a body of glory. We will be released from our physical humiliation, and we will enter into the Lord's glory.

This is the physical transformation for which Paul is aiming, and he connects it to waiting for the coming of our Savior, the Lord Jesus Christ. Let's take note that Paul does not merely talk about dying and going to heaven to be with the Lord, which he had mentioned in the earlier chapters of Philippians. Here he goes beyond that concept to the appearing of the Lord and the resurrection of His body. This glorious transformation of our bodies is the final consummation – the final completion – of our personal salvation.

Chapter 5
Hidden in Christ

The truth we discovered in our previous chapter about physical transformation is profound. It is wonderful to know that we will receive our resurrected bodies when Christ appears. But what should be our attitude about our lives in the meantime? Some helpful answers to that question come from our examination of Colossians 3:3–4. This is what Paul writes there:

> *For you died, and your life is hidden with Christ in God. When Christ who is our life appears, then you also will appear with Him in glory.*

In the King James Version the first three words of this verse are correctly translated this way: "You are dead." This translation is in the simple past tense, which conveys the meaning that the death spoken of is a historical fact which happened at a single point of time in the past.

When did we die? We died when Jesus died on the cross. Our old man was crucified in Him. That is a historical fact, and it is true – whether you believe it or not. However, actually *believing* it makes a great deal of difference in your life.

Paul writes, *"You died."* This thought elicits another logical question. If you have died, where is your life? The answer is, *"Your life is hidden with Christ in God."*

Knowing that your life is hidden with Christ in God should give you a tremendous sense of security! If your life is hidden with Christ in God, there is no power of evil that can touch that life because it is outside the range of all the forces of evil.

Jesus, Our Life

Following this revelation of our "hidden-ness" with Christ, Paul then writes in verse 4:

> *When Christ who is our life appears, then you also will appear with Him in glory.*

Here is a very helpful thought for you if you are struggling with weakness or sickness. (Some of the simplest statements of Scripture are the most profound, and this is one of those.) *Christ is our life.* What more can you need than that? The life of Christ is greater than every problem, every pressure, and every infirmity. I would encourage you to say that often, especially in difficult times: "Christ is my life!" Why not say it aloud right now? "Christ is my life!"

Here is another wonderful thought to consider. At His appearing, the world is going to see *who we really are.* In this age, the world does not have a clue as to who we are. We are the King's kids already, but the world does not recognize it. One day, however, the whole universe is going to see us for who we really are.

This is one more reason why we should be longing for His appearing. Our true life – the glory that God has for us – will not be manifested until Christ is manifested in His glory. The full outworking of God's salvation for us will not be completed until then. It is wonderful to have eternal life now, through faith in Jesus. But that is not the end of the matter. It is wonderful to know that when you die, your disembodied spirit will go to be with Christ. But that, as well, is not the end of the matter.

You see, God has not planned eternity for us as disembodied spirits. Jesus died to save a *whole* person – *spirit*, *soul*, and *body*. His salvation will not be completely worked out in us until we have the *whole* salvation *in spirit*, *in soul*, and *in body*. When will that take place? Not until the return of Jesus in glory.

This being the case, we can be content to be hidden with Christ in God for the time being. It is a safe place. The Psalmist understood this when we wrote, "*He who dwells in the secret place of the Most High shall abide under the shadow of the Almighty*" (Psalm 91:1).

There is no safer place than to be hidden in Christ. Many people strive to be conspicuous or to be well known – and sometimes it falls to our lot to be conspicuous. But believe me, it is much harder. I would advise you to be content to be hidden with Christ in God, because there is a day coming when you will not be hidden any longer!

The Goal of Faith

Jesus clearly taught that believing in Him would result in our resurrection. Four times, in John chapter 6, He declares that the end of faith in Him is resurrection. But I want to draw your attention to one important fact – Jesus does not speak about our going to an eternity in heaven, as He does about our bodies being resurrected.

This is the will of the Father who sent Me, that of all He has given Me I should lose nothing, but should raise it up at the last day (John 6:39).

Clearly, to be "raised up" is to be resurrected. Jesus reinforces this same truth in the next verse. In verse 40, He says it again:

And this is the will of Him who sent Me, that everyone who sees the Son and believes in Him may have everlasting life; and I will raise him up at the last day.

We tend to think of everlasting life as the end or the ultimate goal. But it is not. The final end is the resurrection! It seems to me that many Christians don't understand this truth, and therefore they are not very interested in the resurrection. But that is a mistake, because the resurrection is the final climax. Believe me when I say that God is not the author of anti-climactic events. Our bodily resurrection will be the crowning point of our personal experience – and the ultimate fulfilment of human history.

Tying It All Together

Just to add emphasis to this wonderful revelation, let's look at two more passages from John 6 in which Jesus makes the same point.

> *No one can come to Me unless the Father who sent Me draws him; and I will raise him up at the last day* (John 6:44).
> *Whoever eats My flesh and drinks My blood has eternal life, and I will raise him up at the last day* (John 6:54).

Jesus obviously intended for us to know, understand, and believe the truth of the resurrection of the body. Many of us testify to salvation by saying, "I have eternal life – I believe in Jesus." That is wonderful news to share. But why stop your testimony at that point? God is going to raise you up at the last day! Testifying about your coming resurrection may attract a lot more attention from people who are not all that impressed by just having eternal life.

In most Christian circles, the focus has almost entirely been on getting into heaven. By that emphasis, we have, in a sense, truncated the message by leaving off the climactic moment. What we have unwittingly done is similar to offering a book without its final chapter – which is usually the part everybody wants to read.

The last chapter we need to add – the promise of resurrection – ties the story together. It answers all the questions and brings the plot to resolution and fulfillment. That is why it is so important that when you testify to people, you need to remember to include the last chapter of the book. It contains the exciting climax: we will be raised up!

Chapter 6
Union with Jesus

So far in this book, we have been focusing on the reasons we should be excited about the return of Jesus Christ. We are answering the following question: why should we be longing for His appearing?

As we begin this chapter, I hope you are beginning to grasp how important this question is for each of us. I stated earlier that my study of the Scriptures on this subject revealed four primary reasons we should be in great anticipation of the Lord's return. The first reason, which I shared with you in our previous two chapters, is that the return of the Lord will bring about the *consummation of our salvation*, evidenced by the resurrection of our physical bodies. Our "bodies of humiliation" will be instantly transformed into perfect, glorious bodies like Jesus's resurrected body – something to be very excited about!

We also briefly discussed the word *consummation,* which is another word for *completion.* I emphasized that our personal salvation is not completed merely when we receive eternal life, or even when we die and our spirit goes to be in the presence of God. Our salvation will only be consummated when we are resurrected with a body like that of Jesus. Jesus Himself confirms this four times in the sixth chapter of John, with this statement: "I will raise him up at the last day."

Two Unions

In this chapter we want to focus on the second reason we should be longing for the Lord's appearing – it will bring about the consummation of two unions. The first union will be with Christ Himself, and the second union will be with one another. Our union with Jesus and with one another will not be complete until He appears.

Let's consider our present situation for a moment. We have a wonderful relationship now with Jesus, and we have many wonderful relationships with our fellow believers. But they are not complete. Our relationships with our fellow believers are, in a certain sense, somewhat fragmented. Sometimes they continue; sometimes they are broken off. But that is not the end of the story.

I want to emphasize again, as I did in the previous chapter, that this salvation into which we have come through faith in Jesus is a very *complete* salvation. God is a very complete God, and He never stops short of completeness! One important aspect of His completeness will be a total, final and eternal union for us – first with Christ and second with our fellow believers. Could anything be more wonderful than that?

The Wedding Celebration

Let's begin our study of this point by looking at a prophetic picture in Revelation 19:6–7. The description there is a vivid portrayal of one of the greatest events of human history. As we read this revelation of John, let's bear in mind that we are the Body of Christ, and also the Bride of Christ. This passage in Revelation speaks about the moment when the bride will be finally and forever united with her bridegroom in a glorious marriage ceremony. I believe that in many ways, human language is inadequate to describe the glory which was revealed to the apostle John at this point.

> *And I heard, as it were, the voice of a great multitude, as the sound of many waters and as the sound of mighty thunderings, saying, "Alleluia! For the Lord God Omnipotent reigns! Let us be glad and rejoice and give Him glory, for the marriage of the Lamb has come, and His wife has made herself ready."*

The scene described here pictures the whole universe being in an uproar of excitement. What is the reason for all the excitement? It is about you and me – and the consummation of our union with Christ!

If you have been married, you know how exciting the process can be – to date, hold hands, express emotion, spend all your time together, and finally become engaged. But all of this only leads up to the ultimate goal – the thrill of getting married!

There is a union in marriage for which there is no substitute, and for which every bride longs. She may be excited about being engaged, tremendously thrilled about her engagement ring, and happily planning her wedding. None of that is a worthy substitute for being married. I have attended weddings in many lands. I can confidently say that I know of no country or culture where it is not normal for the bride to be excited about the approach of her wedding day. Any bride who is not excited about being married probably ought to reconsider her decision to marry!

When Revelation talks about the marriage supper of the Lamb, Jesus Christ, there is going to be a union with Him which we cannot even imagine at this time. One of the attributes of the book of Revelation that impresses me is that it does not try to describe our marriage to the Lamb. Why? Because in human language it is indescribable.

That glorious wedding day parallels the moment that every earthly bride is longing for. Wouldn't you agree? As she makes all the necessary preparations, her anticipation grows. We see a biblical commentary on this process, where God asks through the prophet Jeremiah: *"Can a virgin forget her ornaments, or a bride her attire?"* (Jeremiah 2:32). The obvious answer is, "No, she cannot." We all know that the nearer the day of her wedding gets, the more she is concerned with the attire she is going to wear.

But the prophetic commentary continues, and God says, *"Yet My people have forgotten Me days without number."* That condition was true of Israel in the Old Testament, and I fear it is too often true of the Church in the New Testament. As Christians, we are the bride of Christ. If we are not excited about what is coming, there is something wrong with us. I am never upset by people who get excited about their faith. On the contrary, I am upset about people who do not get excited – because the only logical reaction to the reality of our salvation and to our ultimate role as the Bride of Christ, is to get excited!

A Time for Excitement

I grew up as a boy in the Anglican Church in Britain. Everything about that church experience was very dignified. The service was often beautiful, and the buildings were very old and ornate. (These old, beautiful churches made me think you couldn't possibly worship God in a building that was less than 400 years old!) I knew all the Anglican prayers, and I could repeat the general confession and the creed. I knew all the liturgies, and in a sense, I thought they were wonderful. However, I would look at the people as they went out of church, after saying all those glorious words, and I would think to myself, "They don't look like people who believe what they've just said."

I remember one Sunday, in my critical teenage mind, thinking, "If that lady over there were to drop her beautiful lace handkerchief and I were to run after her and pick it up, saying, 'Madam, you dropped your handkerchief!' she would get much more excited about her handkerchief than about all the profound words she had declared in the service."

Many sincere churchgoers have the impression that they ought to troop out of church looking very dignified. But my view is that if you believe what you hear in church, you ought to come out of church looking very happy – even dancing and leaping! I believe that kind of excitement is more in tune with the Bible than all of our dignity.

A wise and whimsical servant of God from a past generation once said, "The temperature of the average churchgoer is so subnormal that if anybody has a normal temperature, they think he has a fever!" Please remember, the Bible is a book of romance – it has a momentous climax toward which we are heading, which we can anticipate with excitement! Nothing else can take the place or compare in any way to that exciting consummation.

A Sense of Anticipation

In truth, only the Holy Spirit can give us this sense of excitement and anticipation. We cannot work it up in our flesh; it must be a work of the Spirit. Revelation 22:17 says, *"And the Spirit and the bride say, 'Come!'"* Notice, when the Spirit says, "Come!" then the bride says, "Come!" The deep feeling of longing comes as we are moved by the Spirit of God. He is the one that gives us this excited anticipation.

The more people are moved and filled with

the Holy Spirit, the more excited they will be about the Lord's return. Our excitement about His appearing is one good way of measuring how much influence the Holy Spirit is really having in our lives.

As you are reading the truths I have just shared, you may realize that you lack the excitement I have been talking about. If asked, you would probably have to say, "No. I don't have it."

The point we have just made about the role of the Holy Spirit is a key factor for you right now. He can instill the sense of anticipation you are lacking. Would you like to take a moment now to ask the Lord to change your heart in this matter? If so, let's pray the following prayer together:

Lord, I confess that I don't have the sense of anticipation I ought to have concerning Your return. I am asking You now, by the power of Your Holy Spirit, to fill my heart and mind with the excitement and thrill of the prospect of Your return – and my union with You as the Bridegroom. Thank You, Lord, for hearing my prayer. Amen!

Chapter 7
Union with One Another

In the previous chapter, we focused on the first aspect – Our union with Jesus, the Bridegroom. In this chapter, we will explore the second aspect. Not only will the coming of the Lord mark the consummation of our union with Him – which is first and foremost – but it will also mark the consummation of our union with one another. Paul describes this second aspect with some beautiful words in First Thessalonians 4:16–18:

> *For the Lord Himself will descend from heaven with a shout, with the voice of an archangel, and with the trumpet of God. And the dead in Christ will rise first. Then we who are alive and*

*remain shall be caught up together with them
in the clouds to meet the Lord in the air. And
thus we shall always be with the Lord. Therefore,
comfort one another with these words.*

The Lord Himself

Paul begins this verse with three words; "The
Lord *Himself.*" The bride will never be satisfied
with anything less than the bridegroom Himself.
No substitute for Him would ever be acceptable.
Many forms of Judaism today teach that there
actually will not be a personal Messiah; there
will only be a Messianic age. But no one who is
really in love with the Lord Jesus is going to be
satisfied with a Messianic age – they want the
Messiah!

The Messiah's shout will call forth the believing dead, because He alone has the authority
to call out the dead. When Jesus stood in front
of the tomb of Lazarus and called him out, He
was very careful to be specific. He said, "*Lazarus,*
come out." If He had just said, "Come out," all
the dead would have marched out!

I have the impression that when Jesus returns
He is going to call every one of His believing

people by name. It does not matter that there will be billions of names. He can do it. As our names are called out, we will come out of our graves in our resurrected bodies to meet Him.

Then there will be the voice of the archangel. I believe that statement must be referring to the archangel Gabriel who, generally speaking, is the one who makes announcements on earth concerning great interventions of God.

Finally, there will be the trumpet of God, the catalyst for what happens next: *"the dead in Christ will rise first. Then we who are alive and remain shall be caught up together with them in the clouds to meet the Lord in the air."* There is going to be a tremendous release of divine power. It will be sufficient to lift the entire Church from the earth up into the heavenlies to meet the Lord, there in the clouds.

The Rapture

Let's take a moment to discuss that phrase, "caught up." The word for "caught up," in translation, gives us the term "rapture." "Caught up" comes from the Greek word *harpazo*, which literally means "to snatch out" or "to seize." The

Latin translation of this verse used the word *rapturo*, from which we have the English term we hear today, "the Rapture."

There are many different views about the rapture and when it will take place. A lady said to me once, "Do you believe in the rapture?"

I said, "If you mean do I believe we shall be caught up, I certainly do, because the Bible says so very clearly. However, if you are asking me whether it will be in secret, or if it will be pre-Tribulation, mid- Tribulation, or post-Tribulation, that is another question." We must not be sidetracked by all those speculations and forget the simple truth of what the scripture says – *we shall be caught up*. This simple truth gives us great hope!

Caught Up Together

The Greek word for *caught up is* an interesting and very active word. It is used to describe what happened when Philip the evangelist, right after he had travelled to Gaza, baptized the Ethiopian eunuch. Acts 8:39 says that the Spirit of the Lord "*snatched Phillip away*" (NASB).

The same word is also used when Jesus speaks

about the wolf coming among the sheep. Jesus says the wolf *"snatches"* the sheep (John 10:12 NASB). The wolf does not warn the sheep, it just *"snatches them."* It is a sudden, forceful grab. That is how the Lord will take us away. One moment we will be here and the next moment we will be somewhere else – without any warning.

We will be caught up in the clouds just like Jesus Himself ascended in a cloud (Acts 1:9), *"to meet the Lord in the air."* The Greek word for air is *aer*, which is one of two Greek words for air. One is *aer* and the other is *aither*. *Aither* gives us the English word *ether*. What is interesting to note is that *aither* is the higher, rarefied atmosphere, while *aer* is the lower air, contiguous with the earth's surface. The word used here is *aer*, meaning the lower air. So the Lord is going to come very close to earth, and then suddenly you and I will be caught up in the clouds to meet Him there.

This will be our final, permanent union with the Lord and with one another. There will be no more separations after this final resurrection. It will be a unity which we cannot conceive in this time because of our limited perspective.

Together Forever

Paul concludes his description of the saints being caught up together to meet the Lord in the air with these beautiful words, *"And thus we shall always be with the Lord."*

I hope you can see how Paul emphasizes this eternal union that will take place at Christ's return. We shall forever be with the Lord. But by implication, we shall also forever be with one another.

This is the dramatic climax of all history, to which all history is now moving. This amazing climactic event is to be a message of hope and consolation. Paul says, *"comfort one another with these words."* Many Christians need to be reminded of the hope and comfort that awaits us. I have met so many Christians whose attitude and outlook is hopeless. How can that be? What Paul talks about here is the blessed hope that is set before all Christians. It is with these words that we are to comfort one another.

As we close this chapter, let me ask you something. What about you? Can it be that you feel depressed, lonely, in need of comfort? Has hopelessness somehow gripped you, as it has so many in this age? May I suggest some possible reasons for your battle with hopelessness? One may be that you haven't really grasped the truth of the Lord's return and what it will mean for you. Maybe you aren't truly longing for His return. You aren't eagerly awaiting Him.

If that is the condition you find yourself in, it would be good for you to actively make that change. You can bring your life and hopes into line with the teaching of the New Testament today. You can become one of those who are marked out by longing for His appearing, for whom He is reserving a crown, a gold medal of righteousness.

At the end of our previous chapter we offered a prayer to use in asking the Lord to help us. If you prayed it then, that's wonderful. My thought is that it probably wouldn't hurt to simply confirm it again right now.

Let's do so together:

Lord I want to confirm that I want You to make a change in my heart. I ask You to help me, by the power of Your Holy Spirit, to be one who is marked by a longing for Your appearing. Fill my heart continually with that longing, I pray. In Jesus' name. Amen.

Chapter 8
Humanity's Only Hope

In our last two chapters, we noted the second reason to long for His appearing – hope and comfort that come to us through our union with Jesus at His return. In this chapter and the next, we will explore the third reason why all Christians should be longing for His appearing – it is the only real hope for suffering humanity. When Jesus the Messiah returns to reign on earth, all suffering will be banished from His kingdom.

We always need to bear in mind that the word *Christ* is the Greek form for which *Messiah* is the Hebrew form. When we say, "Jesus is Christ," we are saying, whether we know it or not, "Jesus is the Messiah." Therefore, all the prophecies concerning the Messiah in the Old Testament relate to Jesus. The return of Jesus in glory will usher in His reign on earth as Messiah, and will end the intolerable suffering of the whole human race.

I have traveled widely, through many lands and across several continents. I have ministered to many diverse groups of people – different races, cultures, and backgrounds. Sometimes my mind is absolutely staggered by even a partial glimpse of the total suffering of humanity. I do not believe it is getting any better. In fact, you could argue that it is getting worse. Modern medicine, technology, sustenance, and prosperity belong to a very small percentage of the world's population. We cannot judge the condition of the world by what we see around us in the more developed nations.

Each year millions of people die of starvation or suffer the maladies of severe malnourishment. Most of these victims are little children. And if you consider the suffering of war, ethnic "cleansings," oppression of the poor, exploitation of women and children, human trafficking, crushing poverty, rampant cruelty, widespread hatred, and spiritual bondage – I really do not believe our minds could bear a total revelation of all that humanity suffers.

Helping the Needy

What can we do? This is the question that reverberates in the hearts of countless Christians and non-Christians alike. There is a branch of the Church which preaches what is called the "social gospel." I am not criticizing that approach, because I believe Christians have an obligation to identify with those who are suffering and with those who are persecuted. We need to do all we can that is within our power to help them.

James says, "*Pure and undefiled religion before God and the Father is this: to visit orphans and widows in their trouble*" (James 1:27). This type of mercy ministry is an aspect of Christian service which is neglected in a multitude of churches today. We have committees for almost everything *except* ministering to the fatherless and the widows. James says our religion is not real if we do not take care of those who need our care.

As valid as this is, however, I do not accept what is implied by some who preach we can solve the world's problems with the social gospel.

We cannot. As James said, we must do everything we can to demonstrate Jesus' compassion to those who need our care. But when all is said and done, everything the Church can do will be totally inadequate for the appalling situation in the world today. It will take the return of Jesus and the establishment of His kingdom to end this intolerable suffering. Only the Lord Himself can do that.

Furthermore, I do not believe that a large majority of humanity are prepared to meet the conditions to have their needs met. That is the real root problem. If men and women do not lay down their rebellion against God, they shut themselves off from the mercies of God.

Pervasive Corruption

You see, we must understand that mankind's rebellion brought corruption on the whole realm of creation that God originally committed to humans at the very beginning. This was the tragic result of Adam and Eve's blatant disobedience in the Garden of Eden. Every area of human life – spiritual, moral, physical, and political – has become corrupt. God's view of humanity is pictured in Psalm 14:1–3:

> *The fool has said in his heart, "There is no God." They are corrupt, they have done abominable works, there is none who does good. The Lord looks down from heaven upon the children of men, to see if there are any who understand, who seek God. They have all turned aside, they have together become corrupt; there is none who does good, no, not one.*

This is humanity in its natural condition, apart from the grace of God. The key word which the psalmist uses is *corrupt*. It describes the kind of life that has resulted from man's rebellion and fall; it is riddled with corruption, which has brought untold suffering to the world – hatred, crime, war, sickness, poverty, injustice, and oppression. Furthermore, we must acknowledge (and this is very important) that this corruption is progressive and irreversible. It is not getting better – it is getting worse and it cannot be reversed.

Why am I saying this corruption cannot be reversed? Because all corruption is irreversible.

We can delay it, but we cannot reverse it. For example, fruit is corruptible; it will quickly rot and perish. We can delay that corruption by putting fruit in a refrigerator, and then it will last much longer. However, the one thing we cannot do is reverse the corruption once it has begun. This is true in both the natural and spiritual realms of this world.

Perilous Times

Paul writes about corruption and its consequence in humanity in Second Timothy 3:1–5:

> But know this, that in the last days perilous times will come: For men will be lovers of themselves, lovers of money, boasters, proud, blasphemers, disobedient to parents, unthankful, unholy, unloving, unforgiving, slanderers, without self-control, brutal, despisers of good, traitors, headstrong, haughty, lovers of pleasure rather than lovers of God, having a form of godliness but denying its power. And from such people turn away!

Paul is here prophetically describing the outworking in human history of the corruption that was released upon humanity by mankind's rebellion against God. Please notice that in this verse Paul speaks about people *"having a form of godliness but denying its power."* A form of godliness cannot reverse corruption. Later in the same chapter, Paul writes, *"But evil men and impostors will grow worse and worse, deceiving and being deceived"* (2 Timothy 3:13).

I want to state emphatically that on the basis of Scripture there is only one change agent powerful enough to effect the transformation needed throughout the world. It will only come by the direct intervention of God through the Messiah's kingdom being established on earth. The transformation that will result from Jesus, the Messiah, reigning on earth will be the focus of our next chapter.

Chapter 9
His Kingdom Come

I will begin this chapter with the statement that I made regarding the banishment of human suffering and corruption. On the basis of Scripture, the only change agent powerful enough to effect world transformation is the direct intervention of God through the Messiah's kingdom being established on earth.

Prophetic Pictures

The divine solution we are talking about is prophetically pictured many times in the Bible. One of the most beautiful examples is Isaiah 2:2–4:

*Now it shall come to pass in the latter days
that the mountain of the Lord's house shall be
established on the top of the mountains, and
shall be exalted above the hills; and all nations
shall flow to it. Many people shall come and
say, "Come, and let us go up to the mountain
of the Lord, to the house of the God of Jacob;
He will teach us His ways, and we shall walk
in His paths." For out of Zion shall go forth the
law, and the word of the Lord from Jerusalem.
He shall judge between the nations, and rebuke
many people; they shall beat their swords into
plowshares, and their spears into pruning hooks;
nation shall not lift up sword against nation,
neither shall they learn war anymore.*

We may quote those closing words, *"neither
shall they learn war anymore,"* as a pious prayer
for world peace. But the truth and the reality is
that they will never be fulfilled until the Lord
Himself reigns on earth. It is the establishment of
His kingdom – and that alone – which can bring
about lasting peace. Though I believe we have
an obligation to demonstrate His compassion
for the suffering, we must not delude ourselves

into thinking the Church or society by itself can meet the total needs of humanity. It is not humanly possible, but will only come through God's intervention.

A Portrayal of the Kingdom

Psalm 72 gives us another beautiful picture of what I believe will be the Messianic kingdom. This psalm is a prayer for the king's son. Some believe it refers to David and his son, Solomon. However, many biblical scholars believe, as I do, that Psalm 72 is ultimately a prayer for the greater son of David, Jesus the Messiah. It pertains directly to the setting up of His kingdom on earth.

The first 14 verses give us a vivid description of what His kingdom will be like. In this kingdom, there will be a banishment of oppression, injustice, poverty, sickness and war. In this psalm, there is also a special emphasis on God's concern for the suffering, the afflicted, and the oppressed. I do not think most of us have any concept of how much God hates oppression and injustice.

Give the king Your judgments, O God, and Your righteousness to the king's Son. He will judge Your people with righteousness, and Your poor ['afflicted"] with justice. The mountains will bring peace to the people, and the little hills, by righteousness (Psalm 72:1–3).

There will never be peace by any means other than righteousness. As I have said earlier, there is a great deal of talk about praying for peace. But I think that is rather unrealistic. Why? Because everybody wants peace – but how many people want righteousness? Biblically, we can never have true peace apart from righteousness.

Breaking the Oppressors

In verse 4, the psalm continues;

He will bring justice to the poor of the people, He will save the children of the needy and will break in pieces [crush] *the oppressor.*

There are millions and millions of needy children in the world today, and the Lord is concerned about each and every one.

I like the fact that the Lord will crush the

oppressors. Some may think such a desire is not a Christian attitude, but I will be happy to see the oppressors crushed. I will rejoice when the injustices that are perpetrated by materialism, ambition, Communism, radical Islam, and prejudice are put to an end – they need to be crushed!

The next verses (Psalm 72:5–11) declare that this will be an eternal kingdom, not just a temporary one like David's or Solomon's.

> *They shall fear you as long as the sun and moon endure, throughout all generations. He shall come down like rain upon the grass before mowing, like showers that water the earth. In His days the righteous shall flourish, and abundance of peace until the moon is no more. He shall have dominion also from sea to sea, and from the River [the Euphrates] to the ends of the earth. Those who dwell in the wilderness will bow before Him; and His enemies will lick the dust. The kings of Tarshish and of the isles will bring presents: the kings of Sheba and Seba will offer gifts. Yes, all kings shall fall down before Him: all nations shall serve Him.*

The psalmist then explains why God blesses the poor and needy, in verses 12–14:

For He will deliver the needy when he cries, the poor also, and him who has no helper. He will spare the poor and needy, and will save the souls of the needy. He will redeem their life from oppression and violence; and precious shall their blood be in His sight.

You see, God is going to require that humanity account for the blood of the unjustly slain. This is confirmed in Revelation 18:24:

And in her was found the blood of prophets, and saints, and of all that were slain upon the earth.

Two more verses, Psalm 102:16–17, strongly reinforce the picture of God's care for the poor and needy.

For the Lord shall build up [or "rebuild"] Zion; He shall appear in His glory. He shall regard the prayer of the destitute, and shall not despise their prayer.

When we are overwhelmed by all the suffering in the world, these words in verse 17 tells us what He will do when He appears: "*He shall regard the prayer of the destitute, and shall not despise their prayer.*" When the Lord comes in His glory, He will vindicate, once and for all, the poor and all those who have been unjustly afflicted and oppressed.

Prayers in the Stones

I would like to conclude this chapter by sharing an experience I had in Jerusalem which made the Lord's faithfulness very vivid to me. One of the places in Jerusalem that Ruth and I loved to visit was the western wall, or the Wailing Wall. It is the western foundation wall of the old temple area, probably the most sacred spot on earth for the Jewish people. They (and many others) go there regularly to read their prayer books, hold services, and make prayer requests.

Those who visit the wall make their prayer requests by writing them on little pieces of paper and tucking them into the cracks and crevices between the rocks of the wall. Any time you go to the western wall, you will see literally thousands of little pieces of papers stuffed into the cracks between the stones.

One very windy day, I visited the western wall, and the wind was blowing many of these pieces of paper out of the cracks and down onto the stone pavement floor. I was feeling just a bit cynical as I looked at these little pieces of paper, and said to myself, "There go a lot of prayers that have not been answered."

Immediately, the Holy Spirit gently reproved me and said, "But there's a day coming when a multitude of prayers will be answered in a very short time."

In my mind I suddenly saw that one aspect of the coming of the Lord is to provide an answer to the cry of the desperate, the poor, and the afflicted – who really have little or no other hope. This world system does very little for them. But when the Lord returns this group will be one of the first priorities on His agenda, and all their prayers will be answered "in a very short time."

Final justice, righteousness, and redemption for the poor and needy will finally come, but only through the establishment of God's Kingdom on earth. And whether we realize it or not, we are praying for this every time we pray the Lord's

Prayer and we say those familiar words, "Thy kingdom come."

The establishment of the Messiah's kingdom is what we are praying for. If we care for humanity, if we are concerned about the suffering of humanity, we will long for this kingdom – which will come only with His appearing.

As an expression of your own desire for His Kingdom – your longing for His appearing – why not take a minute to pray the Lord's prayer now?

We have printed it below to make it possible for all who read this book to offer it up to Him:

Our Father in Heaven, Hallowed be Your name. Your Kingdom come.

> *Your will be done*
>
> *On earth as it is in heaven.*
>
> *Give us this day our daily bread. And forgive us our debts*
>
> *As we forgive our debtors.*
>
> *And do not lead us into temptation, But deliver us from the evil one.*
>
> *For Yours is the kingdom and the power and the glory forever. Amen.*

Chapter 10
Redemption of Creation

We have examined three important biblical reasons why all Christians should be longing for Christ's appearing. By now, you are probably quite familiar with them. Even so, I will just give a brief review:

1. The appearing of Jesus Christ at the end of the age will mark and achieve the consummation of our personal salvation. By that I am referring to the redemption of our physical bodies, which will not be complete until Christ returns and our bodies are resurrected and glorified like His.

2. His appearing will bring about the completion of two unions – our union with Christ

Himself as our Bridegroom, and our union with all our fellow believers. Describing this dual union, Paul says in these beautiful words, *"So shall we ever be with the Lord."* That final eternal union will never be broken.

3. The return of Christ and the establishment of his kingdom is the only hope for suffering humanity.

It is the only force and authority capable of ultimately putting an end to war, poverty, sickness, oppression, injustice, hatred, and all the other evils that stalk the face of the globe today. Only Jesus, by His personal return and the setting up of His kingdom, will bring righteousness, peace, relief and deliverance to the oppressed, the sick and the suffering.

In this chapter we will discover the fourth reason we should be longing for the appearing of the Lord. What is that reason? His return will usher in the redemption of all creation. Understanding the scope of this redemption often pushes us a bit beyond our personal situation, which is difficult for most Christians. Much of the time we live mostly within the little circle of our own needs and problems, rarely lifting our eyes to the horizon to understand the cosmic scope of what God is doing.

The True Center

After spending virtually all of my lifetime in the ministry, I have come to believe that much of Christianity is somewhat like astronomy before Copernicus. Medieval astronomers believed only what they could observe, which was the sun going around the earth every 24 hours. Their astronomy was geocentric, meaning "earth centered" – the sun revolved around the earth. In the early 1500s, however, Copernicus declared that this theory was wrong. In reality, the earth revolves around the sun.

Years later, Galileo expanded the work of Copernicus. When Galileo confirmed Copernicus's findings, the Catholic Church had all his writings banned and held him under house arrest for his position. Isn't it interesting that the Church could not tolerate that revelation? I believe there was a lot more to it than just a resistance to new ideas. I think the Church resisted because it liked the feeling of being the center of the universe.

It seems to me that many Christians today are still trapped in that kind of mindset – that everything revolves around them. The truth of the matter is quite the opposite. Jesus Christ, the *"Sun of Righteousness"* (Malachi 4:2), does not revolve around us. We revolve around Him – and He is the Sun that never sets.

What is important is not what we want or what we think. Our problems and ambitions are not the center of the universe. His will, His purpose, and His priorities are the center. In much of the Christian world today, there needs to be a mental revolution just as profound as the transition from medieval astronomy to the Copernican system, which put the Sun at the center of the universe. We need to learn to think differently about ourselves. The Sun – the Son – does not rise and set on us.

The tragedy is that as long as you and I are preoccupied with our own needs, we will continue to live in them. The way out of your "need" is *not* to get all your needs met. The way out of your need is to be involved in something bigger than yourself. Then, surprisingly, you find your needs are not that important. In fact, many of them will have disappeared!

Reversing the Trend

A large segment of the Church today has become one of the most need-oriented group of people to ever march across the stage of history. If you want to become a popular minister or conference speaker, just preach to people on how their needs can be met. Isn't that the current trend? Tell people how they can be healed, how they can prosper, and how they can have all they want – and more! Even though there is a certain amount of truth in those messages, if that partial truth becomes the total center, it is out of bounds. What really matters is what God wants. His purposes should be the center of our focus.

What was the first petition Jesus told us to pray? *"Thy kingdom come, thy will be done."* Only after making His kingdom a priority do we ask for what we need: *"give us this day our daily bread, forgive us our trespasses, and deliver us from the evil one."* We must get the order right. We must take our eyes off our own needs – whether for daily bread, forgiveness or deliverance – and focus on the supreme, overall purpose of God. That purpose is actually very simple and basic: it is the coming of His kingdom into our lives and into the world.

Self-centeredness is a prison in which Satan has imprisoned most people. My friend, Bob Mumford, says, "When man fell, he got shut up in his little ego box." It takes the grace of God to break that box and liberate us so we can see and experience His kingdom. The happiest people are those who are not living for themselves; they are the people who are living for others – and for the kingdom of God.

The Whole Creation

Let's relate this issue of center-focus back to our key question: why should we be longing for His appearing? We look beyond ourselves because we are coming into something that is far greater than us. It may not put money in our bank account or bring us a new car, or success, or wealth. But it is exciting to know the fourth reason we should be longing for the appearing of Jesus Christ. It is because it will bring about the redemption of creation!

We need to understand that the redemption of all creation is greater than us and our needs. Romans 8:18–19 introduces us to this idea, beginning with a reference to suffering in verse 18:

For I consider that the sufferings of this present time are not worthy to be compared with the glory which shall be revealed in us.

It is very obvious that Paul was writing this passage out of some experience of suffering. If you read the list of all he had endured (see 2 Corinthians 11:23–28), the fact that Paul suffered is undeniable. In fact, none of us have experienced anything comparable to what Paul suffered. Even so, Paul writes that his sufferings are not worthy to be compared with the glory which shall be revealed. Then, Paul goes on to write:

For the earnest expectation of the creation eagerly waits for the revealing of the sons of God (Romans 8:19).

Who are the sons of God? We are.

You see, the whole creation is waiting for the Church to get it together. That is somewhat embarrassing, isn't it? Especially when you think how far we are from being a redemptive force in society. Verse 20 of Romans 8 gives the reason creation is eagerly waiting:

> *For the creation was subjected to futility* [or vanity], *not willingly, but because of Him who subjected it in hope.*

Whenever you read the word *futility* or *vanity* in various books of the Bible, it should take you back to Ecclesiastes. Do you know how Ecclesiastes begins? *"Vanity of vanities," says the Preacher; "Vanity of vanities, all is vanity"* (Ecclesiastes 1:2). In that opening verse alone the word *vanity* appears five times. The same word occurs 37 times in the King James translation of Ecclesiastes. Why is vanity a major theme of this book of the Bible? Because Solomon was only dealing with the "things under the sun" – in other words, the visible, temporal, and material world. Even though he was the wealthiest and wisest man of his day, in the final analysis, he judged all to be futility. There is no permanent answer or satisfaction merely in the temporal, material world. If anybody could have had satisfaction it was Solomon. But he concluded that it was all vanity.

The Law of Entropy

Futility is not merely a matter of man's subjective experience. It is actually a universal law – totally in line with physics. The second law of thermodynamics, which is the Law of Entropy, states simply (in unprofessional language) that the universe is getting progressively less and less organized. There is less and less power available for useful work, and unless some outside power is at work to maintain a system, it will gradually degenerate into disorganization and futility.

This is particularly amazing to me because even though entropy is an established, accepted law of physics, I never understood how scientists could reconcile that law with the theory of evolution. To me, it sounds like the two concepts are in direct opposition to one another. As a professional student and teacher of philosophy, I never believed the theory of evolution when I studied it. Even when I was totally alien to Christ and to the Church, I could not believe the theory of evolution because it seems to bristle with inconsistencies.

Let's look at the concept of futility in regard to the fall of mankind. When man rebelled against God, not only did he suffer, not only did his descendants suffer, but the whole of creation suffered. This is how God pronounced judgment on Adam after the fall, as recorded in Genesis 3:17–19:

> Then to Adam He [God] said, "Because you have heeded the voice of your wife, and have eaten from the tree of which I commanded you, saying, 'You shall not eat of it': Cursed is the ground for your sake; in toil you shall eat of it all the days of your life. Both thorns and thistles it shall bring forth for you, and you shall eat the herb of the field. In the sweat of your face you shall eat bread till you return to the ground, for out of it you were taken; for dust you are, and to dust you shall return."

Please notice those two statements about the ground: "Cursed is the ground…thorns and thistles it shall grow for you." There were no thorns or thistles until man fell! Man was answerable to God because he was God's authorized representative over the whole earth. Therefore, when man fell, his entire domain suffered. That fact is extraordinary, but it is true.

When Jesus was brought before Pilate after He was scourged, the Roman soldiers put a purple robe on Him and pressed a crown of thorns on His head. Purple cloth was dyed with the purple of the thistle. Therefore, His wearing of the crown of thorns and the purple of the thistle was a testimony that He was bearing the curse which man's sin had brought on the earth. It was also a reminder that because Jesus was made a curse, the earth ultimately will be redeemed from that curse. However, that reversal of the curse would only come about when the sons of God come into their own, as we see at the end of verse 20. Let's pick up our passage in Romans 8 beginning again with verse 20:

> *For the creation was subjected to futility* [or vanity], *not willingly, but because of Him who subjected it in hope; because the creation itself also will be delivered from the bondage of corruption into the glorious liberty of the children*

*of God. For we know that the whole creation
groans and labors with birth pangs together
until now* (Romans 8:20–22).

Identify with Creation

When we, as the children of God, come into
our glory, creation will be liberated. This is what
Paul is saying when he writes, *"The whole creation
groans and labors with birth pangs."* Were you
aware of this fact before now? Did you realize
that our fall has brought this agony on the whole
creation? All of creation has been in the process
of birth pangs to bring forth a new age – the
Messianic age. But the creation is not the only
one groaning. Paul continues in verse 23:

*Not only that, but we also who have the first-
fruits of the Spirit, even we ourselves groan
within ourselves, eagerly waiting for the adop-
tion, the redemption of our body.*

Paul writes that those of us who have the
firstfruits of the Spirit are aware of what is going
on throughout all creation. Inwardly, we identify
with it. A true mark of those who have the firstfruits of the Spirit is that they identify with the

suffering of all creation. Indeed, we share in the sufferings with our own labor pains of travail to bring about its redemption.

Did you notice that phrase, *eagerly awaiting?* We are back where we started with our initial reason to be longing for His appearing: the redemption of our body. When our bodies are redeemed and we receive our resurrection bodies, then the whole creation is going to experience a dramatic and glorious change. Isn't that exciting? This coming liberation of ourselves and all creation is one more reason why we ought to be longing for His appearing. I don't it is possible for us to grasp this truth without getting truly excited.

Chapter 11
Nature's Anticipation

In our previous chapter we pointed out the groaning going on in creation, waiting for its full redemption at Christ's return. We ourselves, as human beings, are also groaning along with all creation – waiting for that same exciting redemption!

Even if you are not excited, nature is! In this chapter we will look at a few passages in Psalms 96 and 98 which confirm the eagerness of nature for the redemption of creation that will come at the appearing of the Lord.

> *Let the heavens rejoice, and let the earth be glad; let the sea roar, and all its fullness* (Psalm 96:11).

It will be tremendous when the sea starts to roar. Jesus said one of the signs immediately prior to His return would be that the sea waves roaring would cause men's hearts to fail them for fear (see Luke 21:25–26). I believe those two passages are directly related.

> Let the sea roar, and all its fullness. Let the field be joyful, and all that is in it. Then all the trees of the woods will rejoice before the Lord. For He is coming, for He is coming to judge the earth. He shall judge the world with righteousness, and the peoples with His truth (Psalm 96:11–13).

You see, there is no answer for the problems of the world except righteousness. Whether it is our personal problems, the problems of humanity, or the problems of this earth. The only solution is righteousness, and righteousness will not be established until the Lord returns.

Releasing Faith

As we continue our survey of the psalms speaking of creation, we come next to Psalm 98. In many ways, although similar to Psalm 96, it is even more vivid – especially in verses 7–9:

*Let the sea roar, and all its fullness, the world,
and those who dwell in it; let the rivers clap their
hands; let the hills be joyful together before the
Lord, for He is coming to judge the earth. With
righteousness He shall judge the world, and the
people with equity* [fairness].

Whenever I read the beginning of this passage aloud, it is almost as if I am helping to set the stage for the appearing of the Lord! When I read that God says, *"Let the sea roar,"* I can say the same thing with faith. If I simply think about this concept, it doesn't seem to have much effect. But when I *speak it*, it is almost as if I am releasing the sea to do its job. This is how I read the Bible. Whenever I pray, much of my praying is releasing God's word into a situation. I proclaim what God has said.

For instance, consider the situation in Israel in the Middle East. There is an interesting Scripture which says, *"For the scepter of wickedness shall not rest on the land allotted to the righteous"* (Psalm 125:3). So when I pray for Israel and the Middle East, I declare this promise into the unseen realm. Because it is in the Word of God and I declare it with faith, it has the same effect as if God Himself said it.

Can you accept that? The truth of the matter is when God's faith flows through His word, it does not matter whether He said it or we said it. Therefore, we can read this Psalm in faith, releasing creation for the coming of the Lord.

Let the sea roar, and all its fullness; the world, and those who dwell in it. Let the rivers clap their hands.

Can you imagine the rivers clapping their hands? I picture the wind blowing across the rivers and foam coming up off the waters like as if they were clapping their hands.

Let the hills be joyful together before the Lord; for He is coming to judge the earth: with righteousness He shall judge the world, and the people with equity [fairness].

As we consider these verses from Psalm 98, here is a challenging question: *Could it be that nature is more excited than the Church?* It is a strange thought that creation somehow understands what a lot of Christians do not understand. Creation itself knows that its redemption depends upon our redemption. And because of that, it is longing for our redemption; it is getting ready to welcome the Lord when He comes back in glory.

Taking Our Position

If you are not excited about the coming of the Lord, you are missing out on much of the joy of your salvation. In fact, you might be living at a level of faith that is considerably below what God would desire for you. Quite frankly, you may be living at the level of your problems, rather than at the level of vision and faith that can lift you out of those problems.

As we close this chapter, I want to recommend that you lay hold of the fact that there is the blessed hope that is set before the Church:

1. It is the consummation of our personal salvation in the resurrection of our bodies.
2. It is the consummation of our union with the Lord and with one another.
3. It is the only hope for suffering humanity.
4. It is the fulfillment of redemption for this earth, for creation.

These hopes should be tremendously exciting to us. What impresses me is how much of God's purpose depends upon us – the Church. After all, we are the body of Christ. God is not going to do anything in the earth that bypasses His Body, because it would dishonor her head, Jesus. We need to rise to our destiny. We need to spend less time with electronic devices and other distractions – and more time with the Bible.

Pause and Consider

As we conclude this first part of our study, I would urge you to pause for a moment and give your thoughts to the theme of the appearing of the Lord. If you realize you are not as excited as you ought to be about the appearing of the Lord, open yourself up to the Lord in this matter. Recognize the truth that perhaps you have let other issues and concerns come between you and this glorious hope. Perhaps you are much too deeply embedded in the things of this world and in your personal problems.

If you recognize that this is the case with you, then ask the Lord for His forgiveness. Ask Him for His mercy, and for a spiritual renewal in your life. Ask Him to help you line up your priorities with His. If the Holy Spirit seems to be moving in your heart as you consider this, then I would encourage you to take a moment and pray the following prayer with me:

Lord Jesus Christ, I believe You are coming in glory. I believe this is the blessed hope set before me. But Lord, that hope has become rather dim in my thinking and low in my priorities. I have given too much attention to other matters and concerns. Lord, I want to ask You to forgive me, to release me from any bondage, and to make the reality of Your coming very vivid for me.

Help me, Lord, to make proper preparation – that I may be ready for anything that is coming on the earth, and that I may stand before You, the Son of Man. I long to see You in Your glory and be transformed into Your likeness. Amen.

If you prayed this prayer, stretch out your faith to expect God to begin to rearrange your priorities.

The Next Steps

Having considered the *why* of our longing for the Lord's appearing, we now want to look to the Scriptures for practical guidance: how do I prepare for the coming of the Lord? What practical goals and activities should I undertake so I will be ready when He comes? These matters will be the focus of the next chapters of *Anticipating Jesus' Return.*

Chapter 12

How Should We Prepare?

As we continue with our theme, *Anticipating Jesus' Return,* we need to realize again that it is a theme that can radically change our entire focus in life. At the heart of the matter is one penetrating question you and I must answer: Are we longing for the appearing of the Lord?

This question came to me as I was meditating on the basic text for our study, 2 Timothy 4:8. The setting for that verse penned by the apostle Paul is that he is near the close of his life and in prison. He writes these words to Timothy:

Finally, there is laid up for me the crown of righteousness, which the Lord, the righteous Judge, will give to me on that Day, and not to me only but also to all who have loved His appearing.

In this passage, Paul infers that within the total Christian community there is a special group of believers identified as those *"who have loved His appearing."* (The New International Version translates this phrase: *"who have longed for His appearing."*) For that special group God has a special honor, which is the crown of righteousness. This realization confronted me with the question all of us, as believers, must face: *Are we longing for His appearing?* And if not, why not?

Through the course of my study, on the subject I settled upon four biblical reasons why every Christian should be longing for the appearing of the Lord Jesus Christ. We covered these points in previous chapters, but let's review these reasons again briefly:

First, the appearing of Jesus in glory will bring about the consummation of our personal salvation. By this I am referring to the transformation of our physical body into a glorified form like that of Christ, which will complete the salvation process for each of us.

Second, the appearing of the Lord Jesus will bring about the most climactic event in all of history. It will bring the final consummation of our union, both with Jesus as our Bridegroom in the marriage supper, and our union with one another as brothers and sisters. Paul says, in light of these unions, *"So shall we be ever with the Lord."* After that magnificent event, there will be no more separation but instead, a total, wonderful union throughout eternal ages.

Third, I suggested that the establishment of Jesus' kingdom is the only hope for suffering humanity. Only His kingdom can end the untold, unimaginable suffering of the human race at this time – the wars, sickness, poverty, oppression, crime, hatred, and violence – all the evils with which our race is plagued. The Church can give a wonderful demonstration of Christian love, but the Church cannot, without the return of Christ, establish His kingdom on earth. The establishment of His kingdom will only be brought about by the personal appearing of the Messiah, Jesus.

The fourth reason (which takes us outside of the limits of our own personal interests) is that only at the appearing of the Lord Jesus will creation be released from the bondage of corruption and futility, brought upon it by the fall of man. For these four reasons every believer should be longing for the appearing of the Lord Jesus.

As we acknowledge the truth of these four points, it would be reasonable to ask ourselves yet another probing question: if we are truly longing for the appearing of the Lord, what will we do about it? It is not enough just to say we are yearning for Christ's return. That longing should be demonstrated in the way we live our lives.

From my study of the Scriptures, I believe there are at least four practical ways in which our longing for His return will cause us to live in a manner that is different from those who are not eagerly awaiting His appearing. In this section and the rest of the chapters of this book, we will deal with each of these four practical points.

Personal Holiness

It only makes sense that if we are eagerly anticipating the coming of the Lord, you and I would make changes in our lives to prepare for that event. What is the first area of focus for us?

A good place to look for the answer to that question would be in the lives of the apostles. As I have read the New Testament, I have discovered that the greatest single motivation for holiness of life among the early believers was the anticipation of the Lord's return. Personal longing for His appearing will lead us to cultivate personal holiness. My own conviction and observation is that where Christians are not living in eager anticipation of the Lord's return, the emphasis on holiness is much less than what we find in the New Testament.

The following four Scriptures are very powerful and clearly speak for themselves, so I will not dwell on them in detail. You will see, however, that in every one of these Scriptures it is the anticipation of the Lord's return that is the basic motive for true holiness.

Let's first look at Titus 2:11–14. We referenced this passage in a previous section, but it is worth reading again.

> *For the grace of God that brings salvation has appeared to all men, teaching us that, denying*

ungodliness and worldly lusts, we should live soberly, righteously, and godly in the present age (Titus 2:11–12).

As I pointed out earlier, grace is free but it is not cheap. We cannot do anything to earn it. But when we receive it, it places obligations upon us. One lesson grace teaches us is that we must live a certain kind of life – *"soberly, righteously, and godly in the present age."*

Then, in the next verse, Paul states the precise motive for this type of life:

Looking for the blessed hope and glorious appearing of our great God and savior Jesus Christ (Titus 2:13).

What is our motivation for holiness? It is the anticipation of the appearing of the Lord Jesus. Then Paul says this, concerning Jesus:

Who gave Himself for us, that He might redeem us from every lawless deed and purify for Himself His own special people, zealous for good works (Titus 2:14).

Clearly, what the passages confirm is that the redeemed of the Lord are a special kind of people. What marks them out? The fact that they are zealous for good works, eager to do their best in every area of life.

Blameless Hearts

In 1 Thessalonians 3:12–13, Paul writes this prayer:

> *And may the Lord make you increase and abound in love to one another and to all, just as we do to you, so that He may establish your hearts blameless in holiness before our God and Father, at the coming of our Lord Jesus Christ with all His saints.*

Our hearts are to be established blameless in holiness, which is a very high standard. But this holiness takes place because we stand in full view of the coming of our Lord Jesus Christ with all His saints. What this passage suggests to me is that when Christ appears and gathers all His saints to Himself in their resurrection bodies, every one of us will be exposed to the universe. The level of holiness in our lives will be evident to all.

Paul returns to this theme again and again, especially in the epistles to the Thessalonians.

When Jesus returns there is going to be some manner in which the level of holiness of every Christian is going to be revealed to the universe. That's a thought that should challenge us!

In 2 Peter 3:11–14, Peter addresses the theme of our anticipation of the Lord's return, which he calls the *"day of the Lord."* He begins with a compelling thought:

> *Therefore, since all these things* [the material world] *will be dissolved, what manner of persons ought you to be…?*

All material things will ultimately be dissolved. All that we see around us that seems so solid and so permanent – the mountains, the great stone buildings, the cathedrals, the mighty locomotives, the ocean liners, the airplanes – they are all destined to perish. We tend to think of the material and physical as that which is real. However, the Bible tells us that it is merely temporary. The "things" that are truly real are the invisible – the spiritual and the eternal.

Alexander the Great conquered the known ancient world in ten years, which was perhaps the most rapid and total conquest in military history. However, he died of a fever at the age of 33. His last command was that when he was laid out for burial, all his soldiers were to file past his body. As they did so, they were to observe the fact that his outstretched hands were positioned palms upward – totally empty. What was the lesson Alexander wanted them to receive? *He could take nothing with him.*

The Basic Requirements

Remember Peter's question about what manner of persons we should be? Peter answers his own question below:

> *In holy conduct and godliness, looking for and hastening the coming of the day of God, because of which the heavens will be dissolved, being on fire, and the elements will melt with fervent heat? Nevertheless we, according to His promise, look for new heavens and a new earth in which righteousness dwells. Therefore, beloved, looking forward to these things, be diligent to be found by Him in peace, without spot and blameless* (2 Peter 3:11–14).

In these verses, Peter outlines three basic requirements for being ready for the Lord.

Being In Peace

First of all, Peter recommends there should be no ruptured relationships which need to be healed. This is very important.

Shortly after my 70th birthday there came to my mind a time when another minister had been very critical of me. We had never resolved our issues. So I wrote him a handwritten, confidential, personal letter in which I expressed that even though I anticipated many more years of active service, I did not want to be called home and leave any unfinished business. Therefore, I wanted to make sure there was nothing between us. Quite quickly, I received a likewise handwritten letter in which he gave me that assurance.

I have made a personal effort to be sure that I have as few ruptured relationships as possible in my Christian walk. Ruth and I have always maintained a little section in our prayer list for relationships that needed repair. I can testify that we have been able to cross off most of the names from that list. God moved in a wonderful way to heal those relationships.

You and I are charged to do everything in our power to be found in peace, without any quarreling, and without any unresolved complaints or bitterness. Most of us have at least one or two damaged relationships. The Bible makes it clear that it is not always possible to bring peace in every relationship. However, it also states that as much as it is in us to do so, we should live at peace with all men. We should take that instruction very seriously.

Without Spot

The second basic requirement Peter cites is that we are to be *without spot*. I believe this refers to the garment of righteousness which Christ has given us. Whenever we sin, that sin is like a spot on our garment. However, the wonderful truth about being a Christian is we know how to get our garment cleaned. We have a marvelous cleaning fluid that cleans all garments as if there never was a stain. Do you know what it is? The blood of Jesus. *"If we confess our sins He is faithful and just to forgive us and to cleanse us"* (1 John 1:9). It is very important that when you and I sin and the Holy Spirit convicts us, we repent, confess our sins, and receive by faith the cleansing that comes from Jesus through His blood.

Somebody has said it pays to keep short accounts with God. I agree with that. Do not build up a big account of unconfessed sin – because the bigger it gets, the harder it is to get back to God.

Blameless

Third, Peter says we are to be *blameless*. I understand that to mean there is nothing we ought to have done and could have done that we have left undone. We have been faithful in every duty that was within our power to fulfill.

Requirements like these three, then, are our obligations in light of the coming of the Lord and our gathering together to Him. We are going to appear in glory – but it is going to be very public, and the whole universe will see us.

Please meditate on those three requirements for a moment – *being in peace, without spot,* and *blameless.* When Peter says "be diligent" I think you would have to agree that it takes diligence to attain these goals. We will not attain them through careless or sloppy living. It will take our genuine attention to such spiritual issues as these.

Dazzling Purity

As we envisage the return of the Lord, we want to look at a final Scripture – that relates to the requirements of personal holiness.

> *Beloved, now we are children of God; and it has not yet been revealed what we shall be, but we know that when He is revealed, we shall be like Him, for we shall see Him as He is* (1 John 3:2–3).

When John writes that *"we shall be like Him,"* he is referring to our resurrection body. In other words, when we see Jesus we will have the same kind of body which He has. Then John continues:

> *And everyone who has this hope in Him purifies himself, just as He is pure.*

Those who truly hope to see Jesus and long to be transformed into His likeness will purify themselves. If I were your pastor and saw that you paid no attention to purifying yourself in your daily living, it would lead me to a logical conclusion and a necessary action. I would have to say to you that you do not really expect to see the Lord. You may say "yes" to the doctrines of His appearing – but it would not be real in your experience, because *"everyone who has this hope in Him purifies himself."* Seeking purity is a mark of the person who genuinely hopes for His return.

Radiant Attire

Let's think about this logically. If you and I are going to be exposed to the total glory of heaven in the presence of God the Father and Jesus and the holy angels, we certainly need purity. That dazzling light is going to reveal every spot on our garments. It is going to reveal any defect or flaw in our character. This presents us with an enormous challenge!

We cannot afford to be lazy or negligent by missing out on our Christian duties. We must be faithful in the small things as well as in the great things. If we are not faithful in the small things the Lord has told us to do, we will not be faithful in the great things. Do not wait for some great task and say, "When God gives me that great task I will be faithful." If that is your perspective, the Lord will never give that great task to you. First, you must prove yourself faithful in the smaller tasks. Regard each little act as a thread in your garment, and you will be promoted. But, more important still, you will be radiantly attired in glory.

All of this kind of behavior represents the first practical way we prepare for the Lord's return – personal holiness. In our next chapter, we will cover the second practical activity for preparation – completing our assignment.

Chapter 13
Completing Our Assignment

In the introduction to our previous chapter, I pointed out the first of four ways to prepare for the Lord's coming – personal holiness. This chapter will deal with the second way we should be preparing for the return of Jesus. We get ourselves ready by completing our assigned task. That may sound very "works" oriented, but God has more than that in mind.

To illustrate what I mean, let's look at what Paul writes in Ephesians 2:10: *"For we are His [God's] workmanship."* The Greek word for "workmanship" is *poeima*, from which we get the English word "poem." This term does not refer to something which is easily constructed – it speaks of a masterpiece. *We are God's creative masterpiece.*

It blesses me to think that when God wanted to demonstrate to the entire universe what kind of masterpiece He could make, He went to the scrap heap for His materials. It was as if He were saying: "Do you see what I can do with lives that are broken, stained, and out of harmony? Out of those lives I can make what will be my signature piece throughout eternity." You and I are God's masterpiece!

In the same verse, Paul continues, *"Created in Christ Jesus for good works which God prepared beforehand that we should walk in them."*

Each one of us is created in Christ Jesus for specific good works, which are our assigned tasks. The truth is, it is not left to us to decide what *we* are going to do. We need to find out what *God* has prepared for us to do. He has a prepared task for every one of us. Over the years I have observed that the most satisfied and fulfilled Christians are those who are walking in their assigned task.

Preparing In Advance

Even though we have already discussed this in Revelation 19, we want to look again at one characteristic of the bride:

Let us be glad and rejoice and give Him glory, for the marriage of the Lamb has come, and His wife has made herself ready (Revelation 19:7).

Please notice that the bride must make herself ready. God does not do that for her. He provides her with the means, but she must prepare herself. When the Lord comes, the bride will be ready. She will not be *making* herself ready – she will *have made* herself ready. The preparation must be done in advance.

And to her it was granted to be arrayed in fine linen, clean and bright, for the fine linen is the righteous acts of the saints (Revelation 19:8).

In describing how the bride has made herself ready, John focuses on her clothing. He says her clothing will be fine linen – white and clean. He then interprets the meaning of the fine linen – it is the righteous acts of the saints. It is all the deeds of righteousness which they have performed in their lives since coming to know the Lord.

It would be helpful for our understanding at this point to distinguish between two related but distinct types of righteousness in the language of theology – *imputed righteousness* and *outworked righteousness*. When we trust Jesus for salvation, the Lord gives us His righteousness as a gift. That is what the theologians call "imputed" or "reckoned" righteousness. We cannot earn it, work for it, or achieve it. It is a gift from God to us.

However, that is not the end of the matter. Once this righteousness has been imputed to us, it has to be worked out in our lives – "outworked" righteousness. Imputed righteousness must be translated into the righteous acts that we then perform. We cannot just walk through life saying, "I have been reckoned righteous." That imputed righteousness must be demonstrated by the fact that we are living a righteous life.

Paul says this to the Philippians:

Work out your own salvation with fear and trembling; for it is God who works in you both to will and to do for His good pleasure (Philippians 2:12–13).

God cannot work in us more than we work out ourselves. The limit of what God can put in is the measure of what we work out in the form of righteous acts.

Clothed in Acts of Righteousness

When John pictures the bride of Christ clothed in fine linen, which is the righteous acts of the saints, he is not talking any longer about imputed righteousness. He is talking about outworked righteousness. You could say, in a sense, that the bride will be clothed in the righteous acts she has performed in the service of her Lord. In other words, *our clothing in eternity will be the expression of our righteous acts in time.*

This is important, because when you and I appear in our bridal attire, we do not want to be dressed in a mini-skirt! We will want sufficient material for a beautiful bridal garment. However, you and I are only going to have enough material if we have had enough righteous acts. Think about it this way: every righteous act that I make is one thread in the linen of my garment. I am going to have to do many righteous acts if I am going to have a beautiful garment.

Many years ago, my first wife, Lydia, and I had a lady friend who was a missionary in Jerusalem. She became very ill and hovered between life and death for quite a while. Because she was a godly woman, she was not at all uncomfortable with the thought that this could be God's time to take her home. In fact, she would have loved to go home.

One night, while she was meditating on this possibility, the Lord gave her a dream. In this dream she saw herself working on a dress, much of which was not yet complete – especially the sleeves. She realized that God was showing her that she could not come home yet because her dress was not complete. In the same way for us there are many more righteous acts appointed for us before our dress will be complete.

In Revelation Jesus talks about people who will be found naked because they were all talk and no action.

Mere talk will not clothe you in that day. Only righteous acts will clothe you.

In this light we can understand the intense desire Paul expressed in 2 Corinthians 5:1–3:

For we know that if our earthly house, this tent, is destroyed, we have a building from God, a house not made with hands, eternal in the heavens. For in this we groan, earnestly desiring to be clothed with our habitation which is from heaven, if indeed, having been clothed, we shall not be found naked.

Paul uses two metaphors together – having a building and having clothing. Then he says:

For we who are in this tent groan, being burdened, not because we want to be unclothed, but further clothed, that mortality may be swallowed up by life (2 Corinthians 5:4).

This is a picture of how we will be adorned, arrayed, and clothed throughout eternity. Paul is very well aware that it is possible that we might have no clothing. Our clothing depends on the way we have lived and served Christ in this present age. Our faithfulness in this life will determine our clothing in eternity.

The Task at Hand

We cannot afford to squander our time, our strength, our energy, or our talents. If we do, we will be missing out on something that is eternal. We have to view every duty – every Christian act and every opportunity for service – as a thread in that linen garment with which we are going to be clothed throughout all eternity.

To me, that is such a beautiful picture. In my mind's eye, at times I can almost see that bride. In fine linen, which is like no earthly linen. It is not merely clean – it is resplendent. It is radiant. It shines. But if you analyze it – looking carefully at it – you will see that each gleaming thread is one act of righteousness. Be faithful in small things, regard each little act as a thread in your garment, and you will be promoted to greater tasks. But more important still, you will be radiantly attired in glory.

What will be the determining factor in all this? It will be based upon our completing each assignment the Lord gives us.

Chapter 14
Continuing Prayer

So far we have talked about the first two preparations for the Lord's appearing – personal holiness and faithfulness in completing His assignments. In this chapter, we will discuss the third indication that we are really anticipating the Lord's return – *continuing prayer*.

In Matthew 24:5–13, Jesus predicts a special period as the close of this age, what Bible commentators sometimes call "the period of the end time." This stage will be marked with unique pressures and dangers. Here is what Jesus says about this significant moment in history:

For many will come in My name, saying, "I am the Christ," and will deceive many. And you will hear of wars and rumors of wars. See that you are not troubled; for all these things must come to pass, but the end is not yet (Matthew 24:5–6).

Wars and rumors of wars by themselves are not the only indication of the approach of the end. In the next verses, Jesus continues with other events that will indicate the approach of the end. As you read this, you may want to ask yourself how many of these conditions are conspicuously present in our current world situation.

For nation will rise against nation, and kingdom against kingdom. And there will be famines, pestilences, and earthquakes in various places. All these are the beginning of sorrows [literally, "birth pangs"]. *Then they will deliver you up to tribulation and kill you, and you will be hated by all nations for My name's sake. And then many will be offended, will betray one another, and will hate one another. Then many false prophets will rise up and deceive many. And because lawlessness will abound, the love of many will grow cold. But he who endures to the end shall be saved.* (Matthew 24:7–13).

Birth Pains

Jesus describes all these occurrences as the beginning of birth pangs or labor pains. Such "pains" are the indication that a birth is about to take place. What is going to be born? A new age. The age of the Messiah's kingdom on earth. The troubles and turmoil the world is experiencing are the birth pangs which mark the coming of that new age. It is very important for us to recognize this truth.

If we want to experience the coming of this new age, we will not object to the labor pains. A husband who wants his wife to present him with a beautiful little baby is not distressed when his wife's labor pains begin. Both have been longing for this beautiful baby that is on the way. If that husband has any sense at all, he will rush his wife to the hospital, all the while saying, "Praise the Lord! Now that we are seeing the labor pains, we know the baby is on the way."

Every Christian should respond in the same way to the labor pains in the world. Our response should be: "Thank God! The birth of the new kingdom is now at hand." As unpleasant and difficult as these labor pains may be, these are the birth pangs of a new kingdom age that is being born. Any mother who has given birth in the natural will testify that once the labor pains begin, they will become more frequent and more intense until the baby is born.

I believe it is going to be the same with the end of this age. We are not going to experience a period of relaxation and peace. Rather, I believe the labor pains are going to become more frequent and more intense. This should not alarm us. Why? Because it signals a new age which is going to be born. All of us must realize that there is no way for that age to come except through labor pains leading to its birth.

Jesus used a fig tree as an example. He said that when the fig tree begins to bud and put on leaves, you know summer is near (see Matthew 24:32–33). Summer corresponds to the coming of God's kingdom. We do not need to go to a university or even to a church seminar to understand what is happening. We simply need to look around and see the fig tree putting on its leaves. When we make this observation, we can say, "Praise God! Summer is soon going to come. The kingdom of the Messiah is at hand." This should be our continuing prayer.

Distracted by the World

In Luke's gospel, Jesus depicts another aspect of conditions at the close of the age:

> *And as it was in the days of Noah, so it will be also in the days of the Son of Man: They ate, they drank, they married wives, they were given in marriage, until the day that Noah entered the ark, and the flood came and destroyed them all. Likewise as it was also in the days of Lot: They ate, they drank, they bought, they sold, they planted, they built; but on the day that Lot went out of Sodom it rained fire and brimstone from heaven and destroyed them all. Even so will it be in the day when the Son of Man is revealed.* (Luke 17:26–30).

The event referenced in this last sentence is the Lord's appearing. Jesus remarks that in certain ways, the conditions just prior to His return will be very similar to what they were in the days of Noah and Lot.

The Lord listed what people were doing in

those days, specifying eight different activities. They were eating, drinking, marrying, being given in marriage, buying, selling, planting, and building.

Take a moment right now to ask yourself the following question: is there some great sin in any of those activities? No. The problem is not that they were doing something sinful. Rather, the problem is that they were totally *immersed* in those activities, and had *no awareness* of the judgment which lay ahead. The word I would use for their condition is "materialism" – and this is certainly a conspicuous feature of our present age. None of the activities listed are wrong in themselves; they are normal and natural. But it is wrong to be so wrapped up in them that we do not see what is coming.

A Different View

In Luke 21, we see another prophetic discourse in which Jesus outlines the events which will precede His return. He describes the different types of problems, pressures, and evil that will come upon the world as His return draws near. However, instead telling us to hide in a cave or to feel gloomy, Jesus says, *"When these things begin to take place, stand up, and lift up your heads, because your redemption is drawing near"* (Luke 21:28 NIV).

We who are believers in Jesus Christ have a different view of world affairs from those who are in lockstep with this world. The world is continually agonizing over mounting problems. No sooner have world leaders solved one problem, they are immediately confronted with two more. Right now, for example, the two problems that seem to be occupying everybody's attention are terrorism and climate change. As we will see in our next section, Jesus gives us some answers for such intense challenges.

Avoiding the Traps

In the same part of Luke 21 where Jesus tells us to look up, He also provides some very specific instruction about our prayer life. Let me offer an initial, general comment: we will never get beyond the scope of our prayer life. Our prayer life ultimately will determine just how much of a Christian life we really live.

In Luke 21:34, Jesus urges us to guard against

despair and have a different, more prayerful perspective:

> *Be on guard, so that your hearts will not be weighted down with dissipation and drunkenness and the worries of this life, and that day will not come on you suddenly like a trap* (NASB).

Most professing Christians are not really in danger of dissipation or drunkenness. But the worries of this life are another matter for most of us. Corrie Ten Boom once said, "When I discovered that worry could keep me from being ready for the Lord's return, I had a very different attitude toward worrying from that time onward."

We may say, "Well, it's natural to worry." Yes, it is natural – but God's Word still tells us not to. There are approximately 350 places in the Bible where we are told not to worry! Falling into that trap is something the word of God warns us against very seriously.

What is so wrong with worrying? For one thing, worrying indicates we are living in this earth, wrapped up in the matters of time, having lost our vision of eternity. Too often we give too much importance to issues that are purely temporal, and Jesus warns us to be on our guard.

Then Jesus goes on to say if these attitudes of worry deaden your spirituality, "that day" will come on you suddenly like a trap. "That day" is the day of the closing of the age and the Lord's return. Jesus adds this statement to His comments about "that day."

> For it will come upon all those who dwell on the face of all the earth (Luke 21:35 NASB).

The difference between us and the world is the address of our permanent residence in heaven. Paul refers to this in Philippians 3:20:

> For our citizenship is in heaven, from which we eagerly await for a Savior, the Lord Jesus Christ.

For all the people whose residential address is on earth, the end is going to come upon them with the suddenness of a trap. The writer of Hebrews says that in this world we have no continuing city, but we are looking for one that is to come (see Hebrews 13:14). For you and me, it is our attitude toward the things of this world that makes all the difference. That attitude will determine whether you and I are caught by surprise by what is coming on the whole earth, or whether you will survive to welcome the Lord.

Strength to Stand

Finally, Jesus gives this specific instruction about prayer in this period of birth pains prior to His appearing.

> *But keep on the alert at all times, praying that you may have strength to escape all these things that are about to take place, and to stand before the Son of Man* (Luke 21:36 NASB).

I am quoting from the New American Standard translation here, because modern scholars have accepted this translation as one of the best readings of the original Greek text. To me this is a very challenging verse: "*Praying in order that you may have strength to escape all these things that are about to take place, and to stand before the Son of Man.*"

The days that lie ahead of us are going to demand tremendous spiritual strength. Many who have been Christians for 30 years or more are being exposed to pressures today which really were not so manifest three decades ago. In my experience, I have seen such pressures increase every year.

There are many problems facing young Christians, but neither does it become any easier to be an older Christian. We are all going to need strength to withstand these pressures and stand before the Son of Man. Jesus tells us where we will find strength to stand – in prayer. He says, "Praying always."

By way of a personal illustration, I totally believe – doctrinally, theologically, biblically – in the personal return in glory of the Lord Jesus Christ. The truth is, however, I can believe it doctrinally and theologically, and yet find that it can be very distant from my daily thinking. How do I remedy this dilemma? By spending time in God's Word and in prayer. I believe that the best way for you and me to live in constant, anticipation of the Lord's return is to shut ourselves in as often as possible with the Lord – through His Word and through prayer.

I will always maintain the doctrinal stand. But my personal life attitude is contingent upon my prayer life. I believe that is what the Scripture teaches. Jesus said to be alert and to pray continually that you may have the strength to escape, and to stand before the Son of Man. This is the third act of preparation in anticipation of being in the Lord's presence at His return. In our next chapter we will go on to look at the fourth aspect of that preparation.

Chapter 15
Hastening His Return

In the previous chapters, we have stressed the importance of personal holiness, completing His assignment for us, and continuing strong in prayer. The fourth practical requirement of longing for His appearing may be a new thought to you – *to speed or hasten the coming of that day*. To explore this concept, we will look again at Second Peter 3:11–12, which we already considered in a different context:

> *Therefore, since all these things will be dissolved, what manner of persons ought you to be in holy conduct and godliness, looking for and hastening the coming of the day of God...?*

The translation of this term *hastening* in the King James Version is "hastening unto." But almost all the modern translations have decided that the correct translation is not "hastening unto" but "hastening the coming of the day of God." The New International Version translation reads as follows: "speed its coming." This is a challenging thought, because it indicates that there are actions we can take that will bring the day of the Lord nearer.

For those readers who are theologically minded, I believe God knows the exact day and hour that Jesus will return. Nevertheless, it will not happen until we have fulfilled the conditions. This seeming conflict is resolved by God's omniscience, because God knows when there will be a generation that is ready to do what is needed to bring back the Lord. My prayer is that we may be looking at that generation. What this generation does will have the potential to hasten the return of Jesus Christ.

The Sign

What is the main activity we can engage in to hasten the day of His coming? I believe the essential requirement we must meet for the Lord to return is stated very clearly by Jesus in Matthew 24 – and it has to do with the preaching of the gospel to all nations of the world.

In verse 3, the disciples ask Jesus some direct questions, which He then proceeds to answer.

> *Now as He sat on the Mount of Olives, the disciples came to Him privately, saying, "Tell us, when will these things be? And what will be the sign of Your coming, and of the end of the age?"* (Matthew 24:3).

What the disciples meant by "these things" was the destruction of the temple, which Jesus had referenced in verse 1. In the verses that follow the disciples' questions, Jesus gives a number of signs – false messiahs, false prophets, famines, pestilences, earthquakes, increasing lawlessness, and the lack of love among God's people. Those are negative signs, but He still has not answered the question, "What will be *the* sign?" It is this answer to the specific request that is most pertinent to our discussion. It doesn't come until verse 14, when He answers the disciples specific question with a specific answer:

This gospel of the kingdom will be preached in all the world as a witness to all the nations, and then the end will come.

This is *the* answer Jesus gives to the question, "*What will be the sign of Your coming, and of the end of the age?*" His response is clear: "*This gospel of the kingdom will be preached in all the world as a witness to all the nations, and then the end will come.*" The specific sign is the preaching of the gospel of the kingdom – in all the world to all the nations. Preaching the gospel is how we can "speed His return."

Standing Orders

After His resurrection but before Jesus ascended into heaven, He gave specific instructions to His apostles. Those instructions were very precisely given in two places. First, in Matthew 28:19, where He commanded them to go into all the world and make disciples of all nations. Also, in Mark 16:15, He told them to go into all the world and preach the gospel to every creature.

During World War II, I spent five and a half years in the British Army. One of the principles that was instilled into us continually was, "Ignorance of orders is no excuse for disobeying them. You are expected to be aware of orders." Another similar principle which was ingrained in us was this: "An order stands unless it is revoked by someone with authority to revoke it."

Jesus gave the orders in Matthew 28 and Mark 16, and He is the only one who has authority to revoke them. They still stand, and He expects obedience to them.

Until the Church has obeyed those orders of making disciples of all nations and preaching the gospel to every person, Jesus will not come back. We are responsible either for hastening His return or for delaying His return by how we respond to His final commission. The only way we can be sure of the Lord's return is by doing the job He committed to us.

Opposing Forces

One of Satan's main motivations is to hold onto his kingdom – the kingdom of darkness. And being well-acquainted with biblical prophesies, the enemy knows his kingdom will stand until two conditions are met. The first is the gospel of the kingdom being proclaimed in all the world as a witness to all nations. The second condition, which we will not cover in detail in this chapter, but which we discuss in depth in Appendix A, is the restoration of Israel to her Messiah.

Opposition to these two items is at the top of Satan's priority list. By all means, he must prevent the Church from preaching the gospel of the kingdom to all nations. He must also prevent, by all means, the re- establishment of Israel. Understanding this second point gives meaning to all that is happening in the Middle East. The furor that persists about the little nation of Israel is totally illogical unless you understand the spiritual issues behind it. Satan knows that when Israel is re-established, his kingdom is finished.

He also knows that when the Church has fulfilled its task and proclaimed the gospel of the kingdom to every nation, then the Lord can return. Satan is angered if even one soul is saved. But losing one soul is not going to threaten his kingdom. Even if 50 million souls were saved in the United States tomorrow, that would not unseat Satan's kingdom. However, if the gospel of the kingdom is preached in every nation to every tribe, every tongue, and every people, then the way is open for the Lord's return.

The Unreached World

It was estimated that at the beginning of the 21st century, the world population would be over seven billion people. Of that population, a little more than half have never heard the name of Jesus – not even once. The real issue facing the modern Church is how to reach those who have never heard the gospel.

The vast majority of American churches will not become a serious threat to Satan's kingdom until they become a sending base for messengers of the gospel to all nations. Unfortunately, many churches do not have this focus. Instead they tend to keep Christians tied down, harmlessly occupied with religious activities which are not a threat to the enemy.

I am not attacking churches, because they do enormous good and keep the Christian faith alive. What we need to see, however, is that they are never going to change the world situation in their present condition. We can only change the world situation by doing our assigned task, which is proclaiming the gospel of the kingdom to all nations. It is by this specific activity that we as Christians can actually hasten the appearing and return of Jesus Christ.

Chapter 16
Keeping the Faith

A re you longing for the appearing of Jesus Christ? Are you ready to take all the necessary steps to prepare for His return?

These have been the key questions we have addressed in this book. My hope is that the Scriptures we have looked at, and the teachings that have come from them, have touched your heart and your mind. My hope is that this book has not only brought information to you, but even more, an excited expectation regarding the coming of Jesus.

My greatest hope is that you are now longing for His appearing, actively preparing yourself for that grand moment.

The Main Points

The first part of this book dealt with the reasons we should be longing for His appearing. Let's refresh those four initial points in this final chapter.

1. The consummation of our personal salvation through the redemption of our physical bodies.
2. Our eternal union with Jesus Christ Himself, and our union with all our fellow believers.
3. The alleviation of human suffering – and release for the oppressed, the sick, and the suffering.
4. The redemption of all creation – including us.

Following those four initial points of why we should be longing, we turned our focus to four scriptural responsibilities we have as we await the return of the Lord.

1. First, we must cultivate personal holiness, because without holiness no one will see the Lord (Hebrews 12:14).
2. Second, we must each complete our assigned

tasks. As we do so, we are preparing ourselves to be the bride of Christ.

3. Third, we must continue in prayer, strengthening ourselves against all opposition so we can stand victorious before the Son of God.

4. Fourth, we must hasten the day of Jesus' appearing by two essential activities – by proclaiming the gospel of the kingdom to all nations and by praying for and working toward the restoration of Israel.

A Finished Course

Soon after the Lord first revealed Himself to me, He made it clear that I was to be a teacher of the Word. It has been my life's ambition to complete the task He gave me – to teach His Word. I have never thought of myself as anyone special. I have simply endeavored to faithfully fulfill that task assigned to me by God.

I am awed and humbled by what God has done as I have labored with Lydia, my first wife, and Ruth, my second wife. He has truly multiplied what He has given me around the world.

As you finish reading this book, I want to challenge you by way of a personal testimony. In 1958, I was a principal of a college for training teachers in Kenya, Africa. It was a very fruitful job and I had won many of my students to the Lord.

I remember one day particularly during that time in Kenya. I was sitting on the shore of the huge and beautiful Lake Victoria. As I opened my New Testament at random, my eye fell on Matthew 24:14:

> *And this gospel of the kingdom will be preached in all the world as a witness to all the nations, and then the end will come.*

At that moment, it was as if these words were printed in letters of fire across the sky and reflected in the waters of the lake. The Lord spoke to me very quietly and said, "Matthew 24:14 is priority number one for My people."

I thought it over and replied, "Lord, I'm not sure that my life is fully lined up with that priority. I know I'm doing a useful job and I've got to finish the furrow that I'm plowing. But if there is a way I can be more fully in line with Your purposes, right now I ask You to move in my life to bring me into line." It took Him about 20 years to instruct me, illuminate my understanding, gain control of my will, and bring me to a place where I believe I am really doing the things that matter in light of the coming of the Lord.

As you read this, you may be in a similar situation to where I was, praying there by Lake Victoria. Like me, you probably know the Lord, love Him, and you may be serving Him to the best of your understanding. However, measured by the standards of the Scripture I just presented, you may have to confess to a deficit. In regard to your preparation for the appearing of the Lord, some priorities may be lacking. Perhaps you are busy with a lot of wonderful spiritual activities – but very little of it does any serious harm to Satan's kingdom.

You may be a pastor or a leader in the Church. If so, please consider how much you and your congregation is doing that really threatens Satan. Are you engaged in some church ministries which are not going to change anything significant in this earth? I do not mean to offend you as you read this. I simply believe this is a subject which you and I must confront very seriously and honestly.

You may be a younger reader. If so allow me to ask you a few questions. Do you really want a challenge? Are you ready to tell the Lord you would be willing to make yourself available to do whatever He asks that will speed His return?

Whatever age you are, perhaps you feel God has been challenging you by His Holy Spirit through this book. Perhaps you would like to make a fresh commitment of your life – to get involved with activities and godly pursuits that really matter.

Maye you would like to ask God to lay His hand upon you afresh, and direct you into something that is really significant. Maybe you feel you could pray as I did on the shores of Lake Victoria, and say, "Lord, if I'm not really in line with Your purposes, I want to be brought into line. I'm willing to yield myself and come under Your guidance and direction."

If what I have just written expresses your heart, I would ask you to pray, from your heart, the prayer I have printed below – or feel free to express the meaning of this prayer in your own words.

"Lord Jesus Christ, You are my Savior and my Redeemer. You redeemed me by Your precious blood out of the hand of the devil. I belong to You, and I want to serve You.

Lord, I want to do what is really important. I want to be committed to pursuits that will bring Your return. I offer my life to You afresh. Lay Your hand upon me from this time forward. Guide me, and work out Your will in my life so that I may find a place for myself in Your service – the very place You have appointed for me. I want to be doing what I have understood from Your Word – working to bring the gospel of the kingdom to all nations and in some way working for the reconciliation of Israel and their restoration to You.

Lord, I don't know how You will do this, but I trust You to do it, because I pray out of a sincere heart and in the name of Jesus. Amen."

I trust that the Lord will direct you from this day forward. As He does, I pray you will one day be able to look back over your life and ministry, declaring, as Paul did:

> *I have fought the good fight, I have finished the race, I have kept the faith. Finally, there is laid up for me the crown of righteousness, which the Lord, the righteous Judge, will give to me on that Day* (2 Timothy 4:7–8).

May the Lord Jesus bless you deeply as you follow Him in faith, eagerly awaiting the glorious day of His return.

Appendix A
Comforting the Jewish People

In Chapter 15 of *Anticipating Jesus' Return*, I made the point that one of the elements in hastening the return of Jesus Christ was the proper treatment of the Jewish people. Rather than covering this topic in detail, which would have interrupted the flow of that particular chapter, I have chosen to devote this entire Appendix section to this important topic. (In Chapter 15, we chose to focus on "the sign" of the return of Jesus – the preaching of the gospel to all nations.)

Our Attitude

In Matthew 24, we have seen clearly the one specific sign Jesus said would herald the end of the present age and His return in glory. That sign is the proclaiming of the gospel of the kingdom to all nations in the whole world.

For all committed Christians, this constitutes our number-one priority and our number-one obligation to the nations. This in turn points to us another significant way we should be preparing for Christ's appearing, which has to do with our attitude toward the Jewish people. Perhaps you have never considered this particular responsibility. Yet it is a very real obligation, one which is clearly endorsed by Scripture.

In Romans 11:25 Paul sets these two requirements side by side – the proclaiming of the kingdom to all nations and bringing a message of comfort and hope for Israel. He says this:

> *For I do not desire, brethren, that you should be ignorant of this mystery, lest you should be wise in your own opinion, that blindness in part has happened to Israel until the fullness of the Gentiles has come in.*

I am sorry to say that many Christians today are precisely what Paul said he hoped they would not be – that is, they are ignorant of this mystery. They do not understand the basic principles of God's dealings with Israel and with the Church.

The mystery to which Paul is referring is the blindness of Israel. However, every time the Bible speaks about God's rejection of Israel and His judgment upon them, it always ends with a phrase that includes the word "until." The Bible always indicates it is not permanent; there will be an end to it.

This partial blindness has happened to Israel until when? Until *the fullness of the Gentiles has come in.* Paul then continues his delivery of God's promises concerning Israel with this thought:

> And so all Israel will be saved, as it is written: "The deliverer will come out of Zion, and he will turn away ungodliness from Jacob" (Romans 11:26).

Forever Reconciled

We see here that there are two requirements placed together in Scripture – the full number of the Gentiles has to come in, and then all Israel will be finally and forever reconciled to their Messiah and to their God. That is the order. The full number of the Gentiles must *first* come in; *then* all Israel will be saved.

If we go back to God's dealings in the New Testament, we see that the gospel of the kingdom was first offered to Israel, and only to Israel. Let's also remember when Jesus said, at one point in His earthly ministry, "I'm not sent except to the lost sheep of the house of Israel." We know that Israel, as a nation, did not accept the offer of the kingdom. Because they rejected the king and therefore the kingdom, the offer was then extended to all nations.

This obligation is emphasized at the end of the gospels – both in Matthew and in Mark.

We see these commands of Jesus to go and make disciples of all nations – to go and preach the gospel to all creation. Jesus has never revoked those commands. They stand. They have to be carried out. But through proclaiming the gospel of the kingdom to all nations, the result will be achieved which Paul speaks about in Romans 11 – the full number of the Gentiles will come in until the gospel has been proclaimed to all the Gentile nations.

Nations

Four times in the book of Revelation, we see the picture of the redeemed people of God being drawn from every tribe, nation, people, and tongue (see Revelation 5:9; 7:9; 13:7; 14:6). But the full number of the redeemed cannot be completed until every tribe, nation, people, and tongue have heard the Good News. Because Jesus gave the supreme sacrifice for all nations everywhere, God the Father is going to honor Him by making sure that souls from all nations and tribes benefit.

That purpose of God stands unchanged. We can delay it or we can expedite it. But we cannot revoke it.

This is why I am personally an ardent supporter of groups like Wycliffe Bible translators. Clearly, an essential part of bringing the Lord back is translating God's Word into every spoken language. The work being done in this regard may not be dramatic, but it is essential.

Comforting Israel

While the gospel is being preached to every nation, a work of preparation, as I said, must be done in Israel. As we look now at Isaiah 40:1–3, please bear in mind that these words are addressed to Bible-believing Christians. They *refer* to Israel, but they are not *addressed* to Israel. They are addressed to another group of people who are told to *do something for Israel*. I submit to you that the only group which qualifies for this assignment are Christians. We are the ones who believe in the Bible and who acknowledge the God of the Bible as their God, and who acknowledge the commandments of the Bible as being addressed to them. This is what Isaiah says:

Comfort, yes, comfort My people (Isaiah 40:1).

The context makes it clear that "My people" is the Jewish people.

"Comfort, yes, comfort My people," says your God. "Speak comfort to Jerusalem, and cry out to her; that her warfare is ended, that her iniquity is pardoned; for she has received from the Lord's hand double for all her sins" (Isaiah 40:1–2).

That is most certainly a message of comfort to the Jewish people. It is the message that their long, long night of suffering is coming to an end. It is the message that Jerusalem is to be restored and their nation is to be restored. Then Isaiah goes on:

> *The voice of one crying in the wilderness: "Prepare the way of the Lord; make straight in the desert a highway for our God"* (Isaiah 40:3).

You will see that this message of comfort to Israel is also preparing the way for the Lord. Comforting Israel is one of the ways we prepare the way for the coming of the Lord.

A little further on in Isaiah 40, Isaiah gives us the contents of the message.

> *The grass withers, the flower fades, because the breath of the Lord blows upon it: surely the people are grass. The grass withers, the flower fades* (Isaiah 40:7–8).

What comfort is there in those words? You and I would acknowledge that they are true. But they are not words of comfort. Comfort is in the final phrase that follows:

But the Word of our God stands forever (Isaiah 40:8).

Let me read those two verses again in the light of that final phrase.

The grass withers, the flower fades, because the breath of the Lord blows upon it; surely the people are grass. The grass withers, the flower fades, but the Word of our God stands forever (Isaiah 40:7–8).

Everything fleshly – everything of a material nature – is destined to pass away. But in the midst of all of it, there is one pillar that stands eternal and unchanged. It is the Word of our God.

Why is that a message of comfort for Israel? Because it is the Word of God which promises them their restoration. As long as the Word of God stands, Israel has comfort promised to them through that Word.

The Privilege

I have had the privilege in past years of speaking to groups of Jewish people in many nations, in synagogues, and in other meeting places. Not being Jewish myself, I have always approached them as a Gentile who believes that Jesus is the Messiah. I have tried to explain to them why I have hope for the Jewish people – why I have words of comfort to offer them.

Having introduced myself that way, I explain how I came to believe in the Bible, as a professor of philosophy studying the Bible as a work of philosophy. I tell them I encountered the Lord through it, and came to believe in it as the inspired Word of God. That statement has always attracted the attention of Jewish people, because they respect academic education.

Then I explain that while I was studying the Bible, I came to find the promises of God for the restoration of the Jewish people. I usually end such a talk by quoting a whole number of these clear prophecies about the restoration of Israel.

Here is an amazing fact: I have discovered that at least 80 percent of the Jewish people I have met do not know those prophecies. They are ignorant of their own prophets. Often, a number of Jewish people would come up to me afterward and say, "I didn't know that was in our

Bible. Where is it? Can you tell me where to find it?" What a privilege we have! The privilege of telling the good news of the promised restoration of Israel to the Jewish people, comforting them, and preparing the way for the return of the Messiah.

The Time of Mercy and Favor

As we close this section, let me give you just one of these precious words of comfort. It appears in Psalm 102:

> *But you, O Lord, shall endure forever, and the remembrance of Your name to all generations. You will arise and have mercy on Zion; for the time to favor her, the set times, has come* (Psalm 102:12–13).

When I have cited this passage, I tell the Jewish people that in God's prophetic calendar, there is an appointed time when He is going to arise and have mercy upon Zion, on the Jewish people and on their land. Then I tell them, "That time is now. We are living in that time. God is going to show you mercy and favor. He is going to restore you."

You see, if we take this message to the Jewish people, we can do something wonderful for ourselves. We can begin to repay part of the immense – in fact, inestimable – debt we owe to them.

Let me close with these reflections. Have you considered what spiritual inheritance we would have as Christians without the Jewish people? We would have no patriarchs, no prophets, no apostles, no Bible, and no Savior. It is no wonder Jesus said, "Salvation is from the Jews." My dear reader, it is time we began to repay that debt. It is time to prepare the heart of Israel for the return of their Messiah.

About Derek Prince

Derek Prince (1915–2003) was born in India of British parents. He was educated as a scholar of Greek and Latin at Eton College and King's College, Cambridge in England. Upon graduation he held a fellowship (equivalent to a professorship) in Ancient and Modern Philosophy at King's College. Prince also studied Hebrew, Aramaic, and modern languages at Cambridge and the Hebrew University in Jerusalem. As a student, he was a philosopher and self-proclaimed agnostic.

Bible Teacher

While in the British Medical Corps during World War II, Prince began to study the Bible as a philosophical work. Converted through a powerful encounter with Jesus Christ, he was baptized in the Holy Spirit a few days later. Out of this encounter, he formed two conclusions: first, that Jesus Christ is alive; second, that the Bible is a true, relevant, up-to-date book. These conclusions altered the whole course of his life, which he then devoted to studying and teaching the Bible as the Word of God.

Discharged from the army in Jerusalem in 1945, he married Lydia Christensen, founder of a children's home there. Upon their marriage, he immediately became father to Lydia's eight adopted daughters – six Jewish, one Palestinian Arab, and one English. Together, the family saw the rebirth of the state of Israel in 1948. In the late 1950s, they adopted another daughter while Prince was serving as principal of a teacher training college in Kenya.

In 1963, the Princes immigrated to the United States and pastored a church in Seattle. In 1973, Prince became one of the founders of Intercessors for America. His book *Shaping History through Prayer and Fasting* has awakened Christians around the world to their responsibility to pray for their governments. Many consider underground translations of the book as instrumental in the fall of communist regimes in the USSR, East Germany, and Czechoslovakia.

Lydia Prince died in 1975, and Prince married Ruth Baker (a single mother to three adopted children) in 1978. He met his second wife, like his first wife, while she was serving the Lord in Jerusalem. Ruth died in December 1998 in Jerusalem, where they had lived since 1981.

Teaching, Preaching and Broadcasting

Until a few years before his own death in 2003 at the age of eighty-eight, Prince persisted in the ministry God had called him to as he traveled the world, imparting God's revealed truth, praying for the sick and afflicted, and sharing his prophetic insights into world events in the light of Scripture. Internationally recognized as a Bible scholar and spiritual patriarch, Derek Prince established a teaching ministry that spanned six continents and more than sixty years. He is the author of more than fifty books, six hundred audio teachings, and one hundred video teachings, many of which have been translated and published in more than one hundred languages.

He pioneered teaching on such groundbreaking themes as generational curses, the biblical significance of Israel, and demonology.

Prince's radio program, which began in 1979, has been translated into more than a dozen languages and continues to touch lives. Derek's main gift of explaining the Bible and its teaching in a clear and simple way has helped build a foundation of faith in millions of lives. His nondenominational, nonsectarian approach has made his teaching equally relevant and helpful to people from all racial and religious backgrounds, and his teaching is estimated to have reached more than half the globe.

DPM Worldwide Ministry

In 2002, he said, "It is my desire – and I believe the Lord's desire – that this ministry continue the work, which God began through me over sixty years ago, until Jesus returns."

Derek Prince Ministries International continues to reach out to believers in over 140 countries with Derek's teaching, fulfilling the mandate to keep on "until Jesus returns." This is accomplished through the outreaches of more than thirty Derek Prince offices around the world, including primary work in Australia, Canada, China, France, Germany, the Netherlands, New Zealand, Norway, Russia, South Africa, Switzerland, the United Kingdom, and the United States. For current information about these and other worldwide locations, visit www.derekprince.com.

BE PERFECT – BUT HOW?

In this book Derek Prince points out that perfection encompasses two related aspects: maturity and completeness. Walk with Derek through 2 Peter 1:2–7 as he uncovers each of these building blocks, explaining how to empower you to incorporate each one into the foundation of your life.

"Very helpful and encouraging book. You will enjoy the simplicity and yet you will see great depths. It will bless you." (Customer Review)

£4.99
ISBN 978-1-908594-94-5

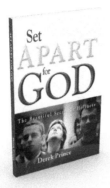

SURVIVING THE LAST DAYS

How do people respond to the fact that we are living in what the Bible calls the "last days"? Some live in denial, choosing to ignore Scripture because it's just too uncomfortable to think about. Some are consumed with signs of the end times, connecting everything they see and hear to the coming of the end of the age.

In this powerful booklet, you will learn about the great, basic problem humanity faces, the essential key to approaching the last days and Jesus' role in the end of the age. As you embrace these truths, you will discover how to face the last days without fear.

£4.99
ISBN 978-1-78263-569-7

www.dpmuk.org/shop

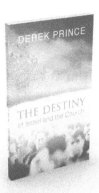

www.dpmuk.org/shop

Derek Prince Ministries Offices Worldwide

DPM – Asia/Pacific

38 Hawdon Street

Sydenham

Christchurch 8023

New Zealand

T: + 64 3 366 4443

E: admin@dpm.co.nz

W: www.dpm.co.nz and www.derekprince.in

DPM – Australia

15 Park Road

Seven Hills

New South Wales 2147

Australia

T: +61 2 9838 7778

E: enquiries@au.derekprince.com

W: www.derekprince.com.au

DPM – Canada
P.O. Box 8354 Halifax
Nova Scotia B3K 5M1
Canada
T: + 1 902 443 9577
E: enquiries.dpm@eastlink.ca
W: www.derekprince.org

DPM – France
B.P. 31, Route d'Oupia
34210 Olonzac
France
T: + 33 468 913872
E: info@derekprince.fr
W: www.derekprince.fr

DPM – Germany
Söldenhofstr. 10
83308 Trostberg
Germany
T: + 49 8621 64146
E: ibl@ibl-dpm.net
W: www.ibl-dpm.net

DPM – Netherlands

Nijverheidsweg 12
7005 BJ Doetinchem
Netherlands
T: +31 251–255044
E: info@derekprince.nl
W: www.derekprince.nl

DPM – Norway

P.O. Box 129
Lodderfjord
N-5881 Bergen
Norway
T: +47 928 39855
E: sverre@derekprince.no
W: www.derekprince.no

Derek Prince Publications Pte. Ltd.

P.O. Box 2046
Robinson Road Post Office
Singapore 904046
T: + 65 6392 1812
E: dpmchina@singnet.com.sg
W: www.dpmchina.org (English)
    www.ygmweb.org (Chinese)

DPM – South Africa
P.O. Box 33367
Glenstantia
0010 Pretoria
South Africa
T: +27 12 348 9537
E: enquiries@derekprince.co.za
W: www.derekprince.co.za

DPM – Switzerland
Alpenblick 8
CH-8934 Knonau
Switzerland
T: + 41 44 768 25 06
E: dpm-ch@ibl-dpm.net
W: www.ibl-dpm.net

DPM – UK
P.O. Box 393
Hitchin SG5 9EU
United Kingdom
T: + 44 1462 492100
E: enquiries@dpmuk.org
W: www.dpmuk.org

DPM – USA

P.O. Box 19501

Charlotte NC 28219

USA

T: + 1 704 357 3556

E: ContactUs@derekprince.org

W: www.derekprince.org

Lightning Source UK Ltd.
Milton Keynes UK
UKHW021814011218
333309UK00005B/59/P